MOMMA *Married* A MAN

GODZCHILD PUBLICATIONS

Copyright © 2011 Halsey & Associates

Published by Godzchild Publications
a division of Godzchild, Inc.
22 Halleck St., Newark, NJ 07104
www.godzchildproductions.net

Printed in the United States of America 2011— First Edition
Book Cover designed by Stephen Reid of Chosengrfx

Library of Congress Cataloging-in-Publications Data
Momma Married A Man/Ruth Halsey.

ISBN 978-1-937095-14-7 (pbk.)

1. Halsey, Ruth. 2. Biography 3. Business
4. Inspirational

2011937495
BSM 55495

TABLE OF CONTENTS

Dedication

This book is dedicated to my daughter, Karen who has always been with me in every endeavor. She has given me her total support and cooperation in pulling this book together. I love her so much for the daughter that she is, as well as my best friend.

Thanks for helping me make this book the greatest book ever written.

Love you,
Mom

Disclosures

This book was written based on my experience as an Independent Business Owner in the early years of the business and contains some dated terminology; even so the impact and relevance of this amazing story and business; the experience remains the same.

Lifestyle Representation Disclosure

The success depicted in this profile may reflect income from sources other than Amway such as earnings from the sale of Business Support Materials or other businesses and investments.

Growth Incentives Program Disclosure for BSM available in both Canada and the United States

The Amway Independent Business Owner Compensation Plan (IBO Compensation Plan) offers monthly and annual bonuses that IBOs can earn in accordance with their contract with Amway. IBOs also may qualify for the AMWAY™ Growth Incentives Program (GI Program), a collection of discretionary programs separate from the IBO Compensation Plan and that can vary from year to year. IBO eligibility for the GI Program is at Amway's discretion. The GI Program is available only to IBOs in "good standing" and those whose conduct demonstrates high ethical and business standards aligned with the goals and objectives of Amway and its related businesses.

The average monthly Gross Income for "active" IBOs was USD $202 (in the U.S.)/CAD $198 (in Canada). Approximately 46% of all IBOs in the U.S., and 48% of IBOs in Canada, were "active." IBOs were considered "active" in months in 2010 when they attempted to make a retail sale, or presented the

Amway IBO Compensation Plan, or received bonus money, or attended an Amway or IBO meeting. If someone sustained that level of activity every month for a whole year, their annualized Gross Income would be $2,424 (U.S.)/$2,376 (Canada). Of course, not every IBO chooses to be active every month. "Gross Income" means the amount received from retail sales, minus the cost of goods sold, plus monthly bonuses and cash incentives. It excludes all annual bonuses and cash incentives, and all non-cash awards, which may be significant. There may also be significant business expenses, mostly discretionary, that may be greater in relation to income in the first years of operation. For the purposes of the calculation in Canada, individuals who were IBOs for less than the entire year in 2010 were excluded.

Following are approximate percentages of IBOs in North America who achieved the illustrated levels of success in the performance year ending August 31, 2011:0.0122

For more details on qualifying for the GI Program and the requirements for good standing, see information on Amway.com or contact Amway Sales.

Introduction
The Moment That Changed Everything

"Ladies and Gentleman, I now present to you, our new Triple Diamond Directs. Help me welcome, George and Ruth Halsey."

Atlanta, Georgia. Free Enterprise Day—1982. This day had come quicker than we thought. The escort picked us up from our lavish hotel, brought us to the coliseum, and served us hand and foot. We weren't supposed to be here. We weren't supposed to know these people. I never saw it coming, not in a million years. There were people everywhere. IBO's opened the door for us when we approached the hallway. Limousine drivers took us wherever we needed to go. We didn't have to lift a finger to do anything.

"Ladies and Gentleman, I now present to you, our new Triple Diamond Directs. Help me welcome, George and Ruth Halsey."

The evening was magical. Everywhere I turned, there were smiling faces. In the background I could hear... "If you hear any noise, it's just George and the boys drawing circles!" We just smiled at each other.

"Poonkie, are you ready for this?" George whispered.
"As ready as I'm going to be," I exhaled. "You ready?"
We just smiled at each other again.

George and Ruth—the first Black Triple Diamonds in all of Amway? I had to be dreaming. George looked so handsome that night. He had on his favorite tie from D-fines (a Men's boutique in Vegas) and I had on one of the baddest Steaphen Yearick gowns you ever did see! It was a purple and white one-shoulder gown that fit me just right. Oh yes, all eyes were on me. This was the life.

"Ruth, can I get you something to drink?"
"No dear, I'm fine."

I looked around at all these people, and for just a few moments, I slipped into a dream - A dream that reminded me about the truth of our story. A dream that didn't happen overnight, but one that included struggles, success, sad times, glad times, and a lot of love shared over time. As disciplined as I've always tried to be, I knew it wasn't me who got us here. And as charming as George was, I knew it wasn't his charm that got us here. It was God all the way. He was there all the time.

For a few moments, I reflected over my life; how I used to walk down the street and talk to God. I didn't know half as much as I know now, but one thing I was sure of, was that God answered your prayers. My grandmother would pray for me when I had asthma, and in the morning, I felt better. If we didn't have money, grandma would pray for a blessing, and somehow, it would appear. As a child, I saw this. I remembered this and realized: if I prayed about something and if I was really serious about my prayers, then God would answer me. So I clung to that belief. I held on to my faith. I may have let go of going to church a few times, but trust me, I never let go of prayer.

It was prayer that brought Amway to us. It was prayer that kept us before Amway showed up. People used to ask me if I saw all this coming, and of course I gave as professional an answer as I could think up, but the truth is, no! I didn't know what I was getting myself into... how could I have known? How could I have even thought up something that my mind wasn't capable of believing? I was only interested in winning the Reader's Digest contest. I never thought in a million years that this would happen to us; never dreamed we would touch so many lives and receive so much attention. Ruth Halsey? In this beautiful dress talking in front of all these people? Not in a million years. I just figured if we were able to win the contest, then we would be alright, I could pay my bills. I wasn't looking for a business. I was just looking for a way to make some more money. I liked nice things and I was always trying to figure out how to pay for them.

"Mrs. Halsey, right this way," said the conference host.

I stepped out of the Diamond VIP room where all the Diamonds sat while waiting for our names to be called. Every time I turned my head, someone was putting two thumbs up in the hallway, or screaming, "Go get'em Halseys!" Everyone rejoiced with us—even the folks who didn't know us. The escort lady—I think she was an Emerald in the business— she took our hand and led us behind the stage. It was dark back there. Cords were everywhere. Technical support staff was flashing lights and pointing us in the direction we needed to go. Every step I took, I was praying I didn't slip and fall with those high heel shoes I had on.

I could hear seas of people, somewhere in the thousands, from behind stage singing:

> *We love those Halsey's, deep down in our hearts!*
> *We love those Halsey's, deep down in our hearts!*
> *Oh-deep deep, down, down, deep down in our hearts!*
> *Oh-deep deep, down, down, deep down in our hearts!*

The louder they sang, the happier I felt. My heart was racing. My legs were shaking. I was so nervous I didn't know what to do. I can't tell you what was going on in George's mind; I was so busy smiling at him. He was so quiet...too quiet! And then they called our names...

> *Ladies and Gentleman, our new Triple Diamonds, from Greensboro, North Carolina. Welcome George and Ruth Halsey!*

The audience exploded in applause. George and I walked out from behind stage, and the people went crazy. The lights were bright, the stage was decorated from left to right. I could barely compose myself. George inched up to the podium slowly. He raised his eyes and showed off that flawless million-dollar smile.

"Thank you, thank you!" He kept saying. But the cheers from the crowd were deafening. They sang, they cheered, and they hollered for what seemed like hours. Finally, George sang the last chorus with them in an attempt to stop the applause: "Deeeeep downnn in our hearrrrrrts." He motioned his arms like a band conductor, and after the last person settled down, he began to speak:

> *...I'd like to say that I did it all by myself, but it wasn't that. I remember when we were out there working the business in our home, and our neighbors didn't know what we were doing. They thought we were*

weird because every night after our meeting, I would leave out with my sponsors and I'd say, "Up your PV!" They would yell back, "Up yours!" No one on the outside understood what we meant. But it didn't matter. I never wanted to put a limit on how hard I was going to work. Man, after we hit Diamond it was a beautiful thing.

The first time we received our bonus I told Momma, "Hey, let's go and spend every penny of this bonus money." And sure enough, we went out to try and spend it. It was hard but we managed to do so after a few days of shopping. You see, when I shop, I like to keep my money neat. Momma likes to carry hers in a big handbag. So when she would pay for her furs and Diamonds, she'd just lay it all out on the counter. Momma liked for her money to be free. And you know, that's exactly what it means to achieve Diamond, Double Diamond, or even Triple Diamond status.

Diamond is being free. That's the thing that is so exciting about it—the freedom. Diamond is waking up in the morning, naturally—that's what Diamond is. You're laying there in the bed asleep. Your body says, "Well, it's time to wake up! You've had enough rest today." No bells ringing or alarms singing. No one telling you where you need to be and when. No pressure about how things will turn out if you don't show up to work.

You're free. And the best thing about it is,
Momma is lying right next to you.

You can look over with your hands behind your head and say, "Momma, we're at work!" You can hunch her in the side and say, "Baby, we're at work!" You haven't even moved. You're just lying there.

Then, you smell the bacon cooking in the kitchen. The housekeeper comes in and says, "Breakfast is ready." And you go out and sit there, maybe by the poolside today or in the kitchen with the big glass doors where you can see the fruits of your labor. You look up on the hill, and there is your sports coach, which sits up on a hill because it has its own runway. Right down from that sports coach sits a Rolls Royce, glittering in the morning sun. It's black with a red accent stripe down the side. Right next to it sits Momma's Excalibur. It's got black fenders with a red accent stripe around it to match the Rolls Royce. This is Diamond. When you can do nice things for your kids and your little girl sits up and says, 'Thank you for being a man who goes out and makes things happen, instead of sitting back and letting things happen.'

Diamond is when somebody in your group comes up to you and says,

'Hey! Thanks for sharing.'
I'll never forget, there was a couple in our organization a few years back. All she wanted to do was be free from work on Christmas Eve. She just wanted to be home one Christmas Eve to get her kids gifts together. And her husband...all he wanted to do was get off the floor at work because it was ruining his health. You know what Diamond is for those friends of ours? Diamond is going over to their house on Christmas Eve and seeing that they are free! They don't have jobs anymore. This is Diamond.
You see, I know a lot of you are in this for the money, but this business is more than money. This business, if nothing else, has helped me to see that Momma is truly my queen. You see, Momma now is secure. Momma don't have to worry about anything, even if something happens to me. Momma is secure. You know why? Because she married a man. Momma married a man. She didn't marry a little guy that when the going gets rough, he sticks his tail between his legs and runs. No, she married a man that would hang in there through it all and do whatever it takes to solve the problem. Momma married a man with guts.
If I can do it, why can't you? We have the same plan, but do you care enough? Have you got guts enough to go out and make it happen? Momma married a man, and nothing is going to stop us. That's the kind of attitude you've got to have. You want to get that so deep inside of you that you're willing to work this business no matter what. Some of you might not believe it. Some of you may not even believe in yourself, but if you don't believe in yourself right now, believe in your leadership. I know what you've got. I believe in you. We have the key to bringing the world together. That's why it's our responsibility to go out and share this opportunity with as many people as we can. And I promise I'm going to do my part, not because I want it for me, but because Momma married a man.

After George got done, half of the audience was clapping, the other half was screaming at the top of their lungs. Everyone rose to give us a standing ovation. George gripped my hand like a warm glove. He turned toward me and stared long and hard.

"Momma, we did it."

INTRODUCTION

His eyes told the story that I will try to tell in this book. We sure had achieved more than we could have ever imagined. Far beyond what my parents had dreamed; far beyond what his parents had dreamed. We weren't just living on top of the world. We were flying high above our biggest dreams. This was the moment that changed everything.

The
Early
Years

Chapter 1

George: The "Junior" Whom Nobody Knew

When I was a kid, my folks never wanted me to go swimming. But I was adventurous so I went anyway. My buddies, Snake, T-nichi, and me learned to swim under our favorite bridge in Wilmington. We couldn't swim at the public pool because of segregation. But that didn't stop us. We just made a pool under the Cape Fear Bridge.

I would always get away with swimming unless someone scratched my skin. If they scratched it, then they would find out where I was and what I was doing because it always turned white and pale if water had hit it.

One time my grandmother gave me a good whipping for that after I got back home.

"George, did you go out in that water today with T-nichi and Snake?"

"No maam," I lied. "I haven't been near that water today." I ran quickly so she wouldn't test my skin.

"Ok then, Junior, take off your clothes so you can take a bath."

The second I unbuckled those pants, out popped a fish from my underwear! I'll never forget that whipping, boy!

-George Halsey

When God made George, He was showing off. On April 2, 1936, George Thomas Halsey Jr. came out of his mama's womb with a mind to work and a determination to play. He never took life too seriously, but he also knew when it was time to buckle down and get the job done. The world knows him as George, but his family called him "Junior." He was an only child and was born in Wilmington, NC. But you really need

This is George's mother, Inez Halsey, when she was younger.

This is George's father, George Halsey Sr.

George always said he grew up in the ghetto, but the picture above reveals his childhood home.

to know a little about Wilmington to get just how incredible George was. Wilmington is the tenth largest city in North Carolina. By the time George came into the picture, the population was about 45,000 people...in one city! It was a big place with a lot of people. But only 35% of these folks were Black. Where George grew up, everybody knew everybody. Even though racism existed, he never really experienced it because he rarely even saw white people. Most of the women stayed home to tend to the children and most of the men worked at the dock since Wilmington was (and continues to be) the city with lots of water. Cape Fear was only a rock's throw away from George's house.

It had to be interesting being George because he didn't have a "traditional" upbringing. First of all, when George's mother, Inez, went into labor, she was only fourteen years old. Nowadays, having a baby that young wouldn't surprise us sadly, but back then, Inez was a baby having a baby. And George's father, George Sr., was only a few years older than she was. So Inez didn't know how to raise George, and George Sr. didn't know how to respect Inez. Just like all these other young couples I see today, those two didn't have a clue what they were doing. They just didn't know. She was a child herself who had to deal with finger pointing, ridicule, and gossip. So her first obstacle was that of tremendous pressure.

The second issue was segregation. When Inez went into labor on that windy day in April, she had to leave her house on the north side and travel all the way to the Community Hospital, passing the James Walker Hospital where all the white babies were born. Back in the Thirties, Community Hospital was the only place that delivered black babies. And if that wasn't enough, did I mention that the child was fourteen years old! I mean, Lord, have mercy. I don't think I could've ever been able to have a child that young. As a matter of fact, I know I couldn't! I barely pushed out the one I did have, and that was during my last year in college.

All that to say, I have developed a lot of mercy over the years for young Inez and George Sr. They were pressured by everyone to get married and that's what they did. It was the custom back then, once you found out somebody was pregnant; you went ahead and got married. They were friends and they really loved each other, but they weren't experienced enough to raise a family. They did it because it was the respectable thing to do. But I'm grateful they did. I am so glad that Inez decided to keep him. I can't imagine what life would've been like if I hadn't known George.

Not long after George was born, Inez's mother left town and moved to Philadelphia. Family support went out of the window. A few months after they got back from the hospital, George Sr. took off and went running up to Norfolk, VA to dodge the police. You see, George Sr. was a bit aggressive. He was the type that would let a woman know when he wasn't happy with her. He would threaten Inez and on occasion, I believe he put his hands on her. So when the police came to town looking for him, he would take off.

Understand the pattern: Inez was abandoned by her mother and husband, and then two years later, she abandoned George. She left him alone in the house for two days with no food or without anyone knowing that he was there. Then, she later moved to Philadelphia and turned to alcohol to cover up her pain. Meanwhile, George's father had already left to dodge the police. As a result, George didn't have a close relationship with his mother or father. Everyone always thinks that sons are closest to their mothers, and daughters to their dads, but I think George wrestled with bitterness against his mother for a long time. He never called her momma, mommy, mom, nothing of the sort. He rarely even called her "Mother." She wasn't a bad woman, she was a good looking woman who had a lot going on for herself, but after she married so young and had a baby so early, I suppose she did what she had to do until she just gave up. But luckily, his Aunt Hazel, Uncle James and Grandma Halsey were living together in the same home at the time—across the street from Inez—so his aunts and uncles found George and raised him until he went off to college.

George never went without. He was the family's pride and joy; the baby Junior that always got what he wanted. He was spoiled rotten:

"Junior, you had something to eat, baby?" yelled Aunt Hazel.
"No maam," George whispered.
"Well, come on and get you something before you go out to band practice."
"Hey Hazel, where's Junior? I bought something for him!"
"He's coming to eat" Hazel yelled from the kitchen.
"Not before I show Junior his new bicycle," yelled Uncle James from the porch.

George had the life! Everyone pampered Junior, and he knew it. He was the only child in a village full of aunts and uncles. Everything he saw was smothered in compassion. Not many other children had two or three bicycles, or could eat whatever they wanted to eat and go wherever they wanted to go. But his folks knew how to take nothing and turn it into something. They were creative and always thinking about how to be better.

I think that's where George's desire to be free was born. George wanted everyone to be free. He wanted everyone to be happy.

∽—MR. GEORGE - THE MIGHTY EVERYTHING—∽

George decided not to travel down the same road as his parents. Instead, he turned into a great man with business smarts. No challenge was ever too impossible for him. Every mountain, he wanted to climb it. As long as someone placed a good challenge in front of him, you can bet your last dollar: George was going to try it. Even as a child, George was good at everything. He was an amazing boxer. He thought he would become a famous boxer one day. He was an incredible musician and his best friend, James, told me that George was so excellent, everyone thought he was going to give the greatest jazz players a run for their money. He was the kid that everyone in town knew would make a difference in the world. But to George, he was just a kid. He's always been a kid—full of fun, innocence, and laughter. When he wasn't trying to be the world's greatest boxer, swimmer, or musician, George was a normal boy with homework and chores. On the weekdays, George would go to the Boys Club with Uncle Melody or Uncle Horace. In the morning, he would walk to the corner store (owned by a nice Jewish family), and buy himself a nickel's worth of ginger snaps. He loved those cookies and he never ate them without washing it down with an ice-cold glass of milk. Now, George might say he was poor, but that man was not poor. Very few people were able to buy a half a gallon of milk every day! I wish I had a nickel in my pocket to spend on cookies. Nickels were birthday gifts to us!

Yet, at the same time, George's love for milk eventually paid off because George never had cavities. I, on the other hand, spent at least $30,000 on fixing up my teeth. I used to tell our friends that I bought a luxury car for my mouth—with crowns and bridges and fill-ins and root canals. George was the complete opposite; all because of his childhood discipline.

On Saturdays, George would rake the yard. He knew the value of doing his part, and George loved animals. When a chicken or stray dog got sick in the neighborhood, George would bring the animal home, nurse it the best way he knew how, and then he kept the animal for a pet. That's why his backyard was always full of chickens, cats and dogs. You would think his name was Old MacDonald because George loved all types of animals.

⌐ A FRIEND LOVETH AT ALL TIMES ⌐

"George was, hands down, one of the smartest men I ever knew. George was also a masterful saxophonist which kept a lot of people from realizing how shy he was...especially with talking to people."

-James Moore

James Moore was George's best buddy from grammar school all the way until George's last breath on earth. George had a lot of friends in his day, but he called James his little brother because neither of them had one to call their own. Those two had so much in common. They loved instruments, they were both the only child in their family, and the older they got, the more alike they began to look! Williston School. This is where they met in the sixth grade, and that's where George's lifelong journey of friendship began.

George was always the leader. Whenever he decided to do something, everyone would follow. If George said, "I'm not going," all of a sudden, the plans would change. George and James both wanted to play the saxophone. But when they enrolled in band class, George got his first choice...James didn't. James had to play the trumpet and George got to play the alto saxophone because their band teacher assigned instruments in alphabetical order. Luckily, James eventually fell in love with the trumpet, and the two became a duo band by themselves. George could just about play any instrument. Sometimes, he'd pick up the clarinet, stomp on the drums, and tickle the ivories a bit; not to show off, but just because he could.

Later, he became band president and his school band ended up performing at the annual North Carolina Azalea Festival Parades and competing in the State Musical Competitions. If he didn't have the parade or the competition to get ready for, they usually prepared themselves to play for a dance.

George would work so hard that sometimes they wouldn't leave until 6:30. James lived across town, but George would give James a ride home on his bike all the way from Wilmington to Rock Hill. That's the George that everyone knew back then; and that's the George we all know now. He was a team player. He never shined alone. To George, success wasn't success until he brought someone else with him.

George was a saxophone player. Here he is posing with his section!
Picture reprinted with the permission of F.D. Bluford Library archives North Carolina Agricultural and Technical State University.

Chapter 2
Ruth - Little Miss Boss Lady

When people see us now, I think they assume that we've always had. The truth is, though, neither of us came up in an upper class family. Neither of us knew what it was like to be rich. Neither of us had a great deal of money, but at the same time, neither of us felt poor. Poverty is not a state of being, but a state of mind. The more you value your family, the wealthier you are.

-Ruth Halsey

While George was a Wilmington water boy, I was a good ole' Greensboro girl. I'm the third oldest of seven, born on January 11, and my mom and dad, Annie and David Graham, raised all of us to be God-fearing and people loving kids. My eldest brother is David Graham Jr.; then there's Mary Elizabeth, Ruth Helen (that's me), Roy Edward, Lauretta, Mildred, and last but not least, baby Joanne.

George's upbringing was very different from mine. I had a village of brothers and sisters. George had a village of people who raised him. I had a loving family with two parents who worked very hard. George had few memories with his father and mother as a child. I lived on the Southside of town and I lived a good life. George lived on the coast in an average Black neighborhood. He likes to tell people that he lived in the ghetto but that man didn't live in the ghetto! They were just like every other Black family. Nobody had a car unless you were a preacher, and everywhere we had to go, we walked. We were lucky sometimes to get a little bus fare for a day or two to rest our feet. But other than that, walking was our primary mode of transportation back then. It didn't bother us; most of us stayed skinny that way.

◦— GROWING UP IN THE GRAHAM HOUSEHOLD —◦

These are my parents, Annie Laura and David Graham.

I often hear people say, "If I could do it all over again, I would love to be a kid." Well, not me. I don't think I ever want to be a kid again another day in my life. Growing up in the Graham household was no joke! It was both a blessing and a burden, but most times, it felt like a major burden. Every time I looked up, my mother was having another baby and dad had to work that much harder to make ends meet. My family was tight. My brothers and sister loved one another, even though we'd fight sometimes. Like any other family, we learned that you will have disagreements but you better protect each other when you leave the house. That's what we did. We learned that love and education were very important. Second to God, education was at the top of the list.

My folks didn't settle for bad grades. That's one thing they didn't and wouldn't play with. Every time I looked up, I was being told about the importance of education or the value of commitment in everything that we set out to do.

My parents taught us a lot about commitment. They were married for over fifty years and they never let petty things come between the family.

Excuses were just not an option. No matter what excuse we tried to come up with, my folks expected us to succeed. Success to my Mom and Dad meant that the kids superseded their achievements. With no degree or a high paying salary, Dad made sure we had food, clothes, shelter and love. None of us were allowed to just sit there in the house and twiddle our thumbs. No, we had to work!

They weren't like some of these parents I see nowadays where the kids are telling the parents what to do. Oh no, if my Mama ever thought I was going to tell her anything besides "Yes Ma'am," I would get knocked back into the 1800's with her backhand. My father was no different. He was stern. He was an easygoing, handsome guy with a charming smile, but don't let that smile fool you! He never allowed any of his children to live without morals, discipline, and integrity.

If there is one thing for which I am most grateful, it is that my parents taught me how to be a good role model for my children. Dad was a mail porter for Southern Railway. Mom stayed home with us, cleaning and cooking every day. Now, cooking was never my cup of tea, but I have always loved a clean house! I got that from my mother. She kept our house clean. She kept our clothes looking good. Even though we were poor, we never knew it. We didn't depend on relatives or the government or the church to get us on our feet. We took too much pride in ourselves to rely on a system. Our only system was God and family. As a family, we worked as a team for everything we needed. Between the kids and mom and dad, we were going to figure it out.

Our main goal in life was to persevere. Where I lived, people weren't defined by their income; they were defined by their drive to achieve in life. We didn't wait for something to happen, we made it happen. Of course, like every community, there were some who didn't care about getting a good education, but they were the minority. All of my brothers and sisters wanted to go to college or take up a trade so we could be somebody. To be an Aggie or a Bennett Belle was at the top of the list. We didn't let racism or discrimination stop us. Besides, we rarely came into personal contact with whites unless we went into town or tried to go to the movies or something. I once was told to drink water from the colored fountain and sit in the back of the bus. Only then did I experience real prejudice...but do you think I sat where they told me to sit? Absolutely not. I knew who I was and I didn't let anyone think they could deter me from my rightful place as a human being.

Above I am with all of my brothers and sisters. Top row is David and Roy Edward. Bottom: Joanne, Mildred, Lauretta, me and Mary.

◦— 809 W. WHITTINGTON STREET —◦

We lived in a three-room house—not a three-bedroom, a three-room house. Everyone lived in homes like ours. A few people lived in larger homes, but nobody seemed to care what size your house was. We weren't caught up in superficial things like people are now. It wasn't about the nicest car or the best paying salary. The biggest question was, "Am I my brother's keeper?" That's what it was like in my neighborhood.

809 W. Whittington Street was the place where some of my greatest childhood memories were born. It was a classic, simple white house that was a traditional style duplex with a living room, bedroom, kitchen and an enclosed back porch. The porch included a toilet and had a lot of space in the back. All of the rooms were a magician's best-kept secret at night, as they transformed into three bedrooms with a pee pot on the porch.

Now, how we got to the bathroom at night, I don't know. All I know is, we made it. It was such a tiny little duplex with tiny little rooms. The front porch even gave us a place to talk to with our next-door neighbors. Their names were the Galloway's. There were four girls and a mom and dad. Our ages were practically the same, and their dad was what we called an "Ice Man." His job was to drive the ice truck into neighborhoods and deliver ice to preserve the food. Back then, we didn't have a refrigerator that made ice cubes, crushed ice, and all that. Instead, we had an icebox. We would place the ice on top and the box would get cold enough so that the food would not go bad.

So we had our icebox, and we had a little potbelly stove to cook our food with, as well as to keep us warm. To top it off, we even had a swing on the front porch! (As a matter of fact, when George would come and see me, we would sit outside on the porch in the swing). Sometimes, Mary and her date would be inside the house and my date would be on the outside. Everybody else just stayed out in the back.

"Mary, move over!" I said.
"What Ruth Helen? I am over! You need to be thankful you have

a space on this couch."

"But my legs are uncomfortable" I whined. "Mary, I'm about to fall off the bed! Stop that!" I said pushing her arm away from side of the couch. Mary I can't even sleep!"

"And if you don't hush up, I'll just push you out of the bed" she threatened.

"But you keep taking up all the space" I said.

"Ruth Helen, hush up and go on to sleep!" Mary said.

I'll never, for the rest of my days, forget that house and that couch. Mary and I slept on a fold out couch every night. She was so mean to me. At night, she would push me off the couch and by sunrise, half of my body would be dangling like a lifeless jump rope. The other half of me would be dragging against the floor. It was horrible! I probably would've been more comfortable sleeping on the floor.

To get away from all of the frustration I dealt with in my house, I really enjoyed working in the community. I wanted to do everything! I choreographed dance routines and I would teach girls how to twirl a baton. I worked in the principal's office and volunteered to help the overworked secretaries. I was probably the female version of George in my school. I used to play the alto saxophone but I really loved dancing the best. So I became one of the head majorettes in school. The show wagon would come to our school and park its "stage on wheels" on the back lawn. I was one of the first performers on that stage. But if I wasn't performing at school, I was singing in the choir at my church. If I wasn't singing, I was playing tetherball (I actually became the city champion of tetherball). And if I wasn't doing that, then I was just having plain ole fun at the park.

✑ *RULES AND REGULATIONS...OR ELSE!* ✑

Like all parents, my parents let us have some fun, but they also had rules. Because of where we lived, my mother and father were very protective over all of us. They definitely did not let us go certain places alone, and if my older brother didn't go, we couldn't go. I remember, as a child, feeling as if I was trapped and smothered. Some days I would look outside and wish I could experience the "good life" like some of the other kids in my neighborhood. But the "good life" ended up taking them places that I wouldn't want to go—some jail, some drugs/alcohol, and some graveyards.

We couldn't do things like most kids were able to do, but I have learned through the years to be grateful for what my parents prevented us from. They did not want us to fall into the traps that were waiting for us out there. That's why they always sent us out in a group. They taught us to look after each other. Mary, David, and I hung out the most until David was commissioned into the military. Sometimes, we were allowed to go to concerts that featured top entertainers of our time; so long as we were in a group and my parents approved. Roy, Lauretta, Mildred and Joanne could never go because they were too young, but I tell ya, those shows were rocking good times!

Except for the birthday party we had at my godmother's house.

✑ *PARTY AT MISS LONG'S HOUSE* ✑

Miss Long was a lady I called my godmother, but you know how it goes in the community—no one was actually related to each other but everyone had the "pass" to whip your children. That's how it was when I was a teenager. At this particular party, Mary and I decided to sneak out and walk with some boys to the bus stop afterwards. They were handsome and we called ourselves having a little crush on them. So we went.

Now...to this day I can't remember those boys' names, but I certainly remember the whipping we got after we got back! When my parents found out that we were out of the yard without my brother, they grabbed the belt strap, plaited it together and went to town on us. They didn't start off with a speech like some parents do. No, the speech was in the strap! The speech was heard after that first snap hit you across your behind!

Mary couldn't stand getting a whipping and I was always the protective one. So, every time they raised their hand to strike at her, I would reach up and stop them. I wasn't any bigger than two floor lamps side-by-side, but here I was trying to stop my Dad from chastising Mary. Every time I did, Dad would turn around and look at me like I was crazy. I was. I truly was.

> "What are you doing, girl?" Dad asked.
> "Stop hitting her!" I said.
> "What did you just say?"
> He said it this time with a little more firmness in his voice.
> "I said stop...hitting her!"

He raised his hand back like a professional baseball player with the thick black belt, and was ready to crack me into left field.

"Stop hitting her!" I mumbled again.

"I thought you said that you wanted to take what she is getting. Turn around."

Zoom! I took off running! In an instant, I was gone. I was very fearful of being punished, so I'd run all the way around my block, pass the houses next to my block, and when I finally got home, I'd tiptoe in the house thinking I was getting away with murder.

Every time I flicked on those lights, Dad would be standing right there in the hallway waiting to whip me for running!

Chapter 3
Together We Eat, Divided We Church

During the time in which George and I were raised, the majority of black families attended church. George's aunt and grandmother loved going to church, so they took Junior with them. And my family loved going to church, so for the Halsey's and Graham's, church was not an option. Every Sunday, we were singing in the choir or passing out programs or reciting Scripture from memory. As well, we went to Youth Fellowship on Sunday evenings, and we did anything our elders asked us to do. But the key difference between George's family and my family was that all of us didn't attend the same church.

We ate together at mealtime but on Sunday mornings, we went in opposite directions. The kids walked to St. Matthews Methodist Church. The boys always walked the slowest because they really didn't want to go. And Mary was always walking the fastest because that's just how Mary was; everything I did she wanted to do better. The walk was a good 5 miles to get there and another 5 miles back home.

Mom and Dad went to Trinity A.M.E. Zion Church. Trinity was on the other side of town. There was good preaching, a strong knit community, and good singing. But it cost too much for all of us to catch a bus every Sunday. So they went to one church and we went to another.

They would always come to support us on special programs, but for the most part, Mom and Dad went to Trinity. To them, St. Matthews was for the uppity Blacks. And it was. It was the place where lawyers, doctors, principals, teachers and Black entrepreneurs went. Anyone outside of this "group" was sometimes made to feel like an outsider.

One "outsider"—I'll never forget—was a loud Pentecostal lady who visited St. Matthews occasionally, when I was a kid.

One Sunday, the preacher approached the pulpit. It was so quiet you could hear a pen drop.

"Kindly turn with me to the gospel according to John," said the soft-spoken preacher.

Right away, this visiting lady would stand up and loudly start to sing, "He is King of Kings! He is Lord of Lords! Jesus Christ, first and last, no man works like Him."

"Would you please, eh hem..."said the Pastor from the pulpit.

"Ohhh, I'm sorry Mr. Reverend," after she had finished the song. Then she would take a seat or she would get up and walk out.

It would crack me up every time she came. I'll never forget the song that lady would stand up and sing. She made an impact on my life at a young age, and never even knew it.

～ WE KNEW WE WERE LOVED ～

Love was an interesting concept in our home. Without a doubt, we were a proud, ambitious, hardworking family. We were willing to work at any cost to achieve more. My dad mowed grass on weekends, and my brother David was a caddie on the golf course. He learned how to play golf as a result and would get great tips doing that job. Mother would cook and Mary would help out in the kitchen. I would plait my other sister's hair, and help wash the clothes and clean around the house. Roy was out doing other things, and Dad, well when he finally got home, he would come in very tired from working on his regular job or doing part time work at Mr. Red's Gas Station. He'd wash his hands and take a seat at the head of the table for supper. Sometimes his folks from South Carolina sent us fresh meat from the yearly hog and cow slaughters.

We were very protective of each other, and shared a lot of love and togetherness; but I honestly never heard my dad say to Mama, "I love you." She never said it to him. I guess that was just a private thing.

Come to think of it, Dad never told me that he loved me either. Neither parent said it, but they showed it in what they did for us. Like for instance, on Sundays, we used to go riding after Daddy bought his new Chevrolet. He rode us all across town and especially loved to ride near the water where he fished. There was a nearby lake which nearly frightened my socks off just being a passenger in the car. But he still took us out there because that was his way of showing love.

And Mama, she never let us leave the house looking raggedy.

She took time to keep our clothes clean, do our hair, and she kept us looking presentable. She was a selfless woman, and this was how she showed the love that I never heard her say.

So yes, we had our arguments, our happy times and our sad times together, but in the end, we knew we were loved.

Chapter 4

Ruth - A Walk Down Memory Lane

"Mama, I'm gonna' go to Hampton Institute!" I shouted as I ran into the kitchen after running a half-mile home from school.
"Say what?" she said as she continued cooking dinner.
"Mama! I said I want to go to Hampton. Miss Dye said I should go to Hampton, and –!"
"You're going to A & T," Mama interrupted.
"But Mama, I thought you would let me..."
"A & T or you can stay home."
"But Mama, Mary goes to Bennett. I could go to Bennett, too! Anything but A & T. What am I going to take there? I want to be a dancer!"

You know where I ended up going, don't you? A&T. I enrolled in 1954, graduated in 1958 and now that I look back, I have no regrets. In high school, I felt a different way about it. I wanted to follow my dreams. I was the head dancer and lead soloist for the big dance recitals; and best of all, I had won Miss Georgene Dye's attention. Miss Dye was the head instructor of the dance team. She was also the hottest thing going at that time. Whenever she walked in the room, she'd make people look at her. I wanted to be just like her! Everything she said, I was going to do. So you can imagine how a girl like me felt when Miss Dye told me I should go to Hampton. I was so excited and couldn't wait to tell Mama where I wanted to go. But Mama knew what they could not afford. She said a word that teenage girls never want to hear growing up: No!

It ended up being the best "no" of my life.

When I got into A&T, I had no money. David had just graduated and Mary was finishing up her second year at Bennett. There were seven of us and only one breadwinner in the house, so it was hard on my father to do any more than he was already doing. I tried to get scholarships while I was finishing up at Dudley, but I wasn't selected for any of them. It wasn't because I didn't have good grades. In fact, I was an excellent student with excellent grades, but the teachers were partial. If you weren't fair skinned or if your parents weren't teachers, doctors, or lawyers, more than likely, you would be overlooked. So I was.

One time I even asked my teacher why I wasn't accepted into the National Honor Society –after all, I was an A/B student and made very few C's. The only answer she could come up with was that I needed more classes. More classes? Huh? I didn't get it. Some of my friends were getting scholarship money and hadn't even finished their last year in high school. One girl got a full-tuition scholarship to Bennett, and after the first year, she dropped out! It just so happens that she was light-skinned with pretty hair, but when it came to sisters like me, I hadn't taken enough classes?

This was the kind of unfairness I was exposed to growing up. Some people got bad news and decided to stay down; others, like me, decided to fight back. Negative actions always inspired me to become better. I wanted to prove to all that I could do it. I was always in competition against somebody in my class. When I danced, some people thought I was "too Black" to be in the group. When I got picked to do the solo dances, I would hear a group of parents talking to their children about how dark I was. So when I came into the business years later, I had built enough tough skin to handle the worst of them. Discrimination was a monster that I became used to as a kid. But the worst of it did not happen at school, it happened in my own family.

∽ MEMORIES IN PROSPERITY ∾

Grandma Olyer was my grandmother on my mother's side. She was a trip. She was prejudiced, light skinned with long hair and she told my mother that all of her children were ugly. Mama would send the three oldest children on the train during the summer to a little town called Prosperity to visit her. Daddy worked for the railroad station so he got us passes to ride the train for little or no money. Mom and Dad grew up in South Carolina and had quite a bit of land. Dad's parents had acres and acres. My mother's parents were middle class but they had a lot of status. So whenever we went down to Prosperity, we were the "ugly children" in comparison to my cousins. If the cousins stopped by my grandparent's home, they would get all the favors.

We would literally watch them get treated better than us. Grandma Olyer, for example, would cook for us, and feed us chicken backs and chicken necks (all the parts nobody really wanted to eat). But when she fed our cousins from the same platter, she would ask them, "What piece of chicken do you prefer? White meat or dark meat?" It was unbelievable! I hated my mother's mother. She knew exactly what she was doing, and none of us liked her.

GrandMa Trannie, on the other hand, was a sweetheart. After we visited my Mom's parents, we would always go and visit my Dad's. She would cook for us too but never made us feel like we were less than the best. Most of her days were spent working in the fields (with the exception of Sundays. This was church time for everybody). She never tried to act funny or partial toward us. We loved to see her because we always received the best of everything.

I'll never forget: she used to give us five dollars to spend while we were with her (that was a lot of money back then), and every year, they would take us to the market so that we could shop. On the other hand, Grandma Olyer wouldn't give us nothing, stingy old thing. Lord knows I didn't like that woman!

One time, she found out we were picking fruit from another man's tree. Just like any other kid out there, doing something we didn't have no business doing, we were eating fruit and having a good time. Well, her neighbor who lived some distance back in the woods, came over to the house and told her that we were on his property. That was it for me. I tried to stay at another aunt's house (who lived up the road) for two days, hoping that Grandma Olyer would forget. But you know she didn't. She never did beat me but she did whip my Aunt Nettie –her "sweet little baby daughter"—We were corrected so much that I promised never to spank my children, but I did. I never wanted my children to know what it was like to be called ugly, so I decided to take the lessons I learned from my family and apply new and even better principles for my family.

Prosperity, South Carolina taught me to take life seriously and to show you better than I could tell you. Thankfully, I can now say that I love every one of my family members, even the ones that got on my last nerve!

The
School
Years

Chapter 5

George Goes to A&T

Because we lived so close to the water, on a nice summer day, I would get on my bicycle and ride out to the beach. I would get so excited looking at those yachts that one day, I said to my grandmother, "When I grow up I want to have me a yacht." And she'd say to me, "Junior, all you've got to do is go to college, get yourself an education, and you can buy yourself a yacht."

I said, "Well that sounds easy enough!"

So I started doing real well in high school. Then I went to A&T in Greensboro so I could buy myself a yacht. But there was one thing that was bothering me...none of my instructors had yachts!

That's when I figured out that something was wrong with this equation.

-George Halsey

George was always a thinker. He was funny, yes, and his presence was magnetic, but the best thing about George was that he knew how to make his mind work for him. If he could think it, he could do it. Good thinking led him through the right door every time. One of those doors was North Carolina A&T State University.

George visited A&T on what seemed to be a random high school trip. It was Senior Day at George's school, and he and his crew-Roland, Roosevelt, Gregg, and James Moore– visited several colleges in the area. When George stepped onto A&T's campus, it was love at first sight. George loved everything about A&T! He loved the classes, the campus, and most of all he loved that marching band! On the day George visited, A&T was playing against Florida A&M. Hands down, A&T was the best around. Almost immediately, George and his friends knew that A&T was the place they would attend.

But this decision didn't come easy. George received a full scholarship to attend Peabody Conservatory of Music at Johns Hopkins University. He was also accepted into Morehouse and a few other top universities as well, and each school was willing to give him a nice scholarship. Peabody was one of the best schools for music in the country. Had he gone, no doubt George would've played with the best of them. But George turned it down. He turned down a full ride and accepted full support from his aunts and uncles! Some people wouldn't have taken the risk, but George was a thinker. He didn't just think with his mind; he thought with his heart.

After hearing that band, he knew that was where he belonged. Above that, George didn't have a selfish bone in his body. He was the guy who made sure you were going up with him. So when all of his friends got into A&T, the next decision they made was to major in Music. George, of course, played the sax, and everyone else fell into place. George became ringleader all over again.

⌒ GEORGE'S FIRST YEAR AT A&T ⌒

The first year at A&T was a blessing. George became the section leader of the marching band—he was the skinny looking boy with the big smile on the sixth row. Then, he joined the Wind Ensemble, which meant he had perfect pitch and didn't need a conductor to lead him. George was just that good in music!

Last but not least, George pledged Omega Psi Phi (along with Fred, Paul, James, William and James Moore) in the Mu Psi Chapter of the fraternity. He was always breaking records one year and then outdoing himself the next. So, during his second year, George declared his major as music and took on French as a second language. Yes French! It turns out George loved romantic languages, and he found French to be an easy language to pick up. His French teacher, Miss McIver in high school, tried to get him to major in it, but George was a thinker. He wasn't the kind of person you could easily persuade, so he minored in French and kept Music Education as his major. Why? Because it was his passion.

If anyone was blessed to meet George, you knew that he was going to be good at whatever he chose. His passion was to become a great musician. So George would walk around humming tunes and pounding on desks so that he could master a beat from Miles Davis or Dave Brubeck. He was a man determined to be successful in life. He had a deep love for jazz.

∾— WHAT ARE YOU PASSIONATE ABOUT? —∾

If your passion was to become a father and take care of your family, George was going to help you do it. If your passion was to become a great musician, George would go out of his way to help you to follow and accomplish your goals. He was a man of passion!
–Ruth Halsey

You know, somewhere in this how-to-get-rich world, I believe we've lost the desire to be passionate about anything. Too many people want to see the riches, but few of us are willing to choose the path that God has ordained for our lives. What are you passionate about? That was what George always asked his listeners. Figure out what drives you to be the best you can be. That's what George would say to his children.

George's success at A&T was not because he was lucky. His success even after A&T—in the Amway business and beyond—was the result of a man who knew what he wanted in life. He never let another "good idea" ruin his focus from his own dreams. He never let a "doe-doe" bird stop him from flying. He was passionate and persistent. I think that's why so many people followed him. Even as a college student, George was so influential that he got his cousin, James Edward to go to A&T and join the band. As a matter of fact, they nicknamed him "Shadow Wilson" because everything George did, he wanted to do. The foods George ate, he would try. The clothes that Aunt Hazel bought for George in college, he would try to match. George was just that infectious. He inspired you to lead, follow, or get out of the way. Then, he would look back at you and ask, " What you following me for?!"

I'll never forget when George and the crew went to Norfolk, VA for an away game on a band trip. The stadium was called the "Fish Bowl," --a place everyone knew because the field looked like a fish bowl. George got in touch with his dad somehow and told him to stop by. The marching band arrived, and before they got off the bus, George's father jumped on and pushed through the crowd asking:

"Where's Junior? Anyone seen Junior?"

"Don't know a Junior on this bus, buddy. You've got the wrong team," said one of the drummers in the front.

"No, no! My boy is definitely on this bus."

"Your boy huh? Well, what's your boy's real name? Or is Junior his name?"

"George...George Halsey. You know that guy?"

"Of course!" yelled the entire front section of the bus. "George, your dad is up in the front looking for you."

The reunion scene was better than any movie could depict. It was clear that George Sr. loved Junior and Junior loved George Sr. They embraced for what seemed like hours. George was so excited to see his dad that he could hardly stop smiling. The guys were shocked to see this because all they knew about George was Grandma Halsey and his aunts and uncles. George's friends realized that his dad and his family in Wilmington loved him. George did hold ill feelings toward his father because he seldom saw him, but he tried not to show it.

Its members included: *seated, first row:* Carlton Boyd, keeper of peace; Samuel Simons, Eugene Truesdale, Milliard Rutherford, James A. Dobson, editor to the *Oracle; second row:* James Moore, assistant keeper of finance; George Edwards, historian; Ervin Cogdell, vice-basileus; Eugene A. Preston, Jr., basileus; Charles Alston, keeper of records and seal; Coolidge McCoy, dean of pledgees; Leon Martin, keeper of finance; Spurgeon Fitts; *third row:* Bernard Overton, George Halsey, Bernie McLone, William Watermann, assistant keeper of records and seal; Walter McAllister, James Israel, Paul Faucette, assistant chaplain; William Cassidy, Charles Summers, assistant dean of pledgees, and Clemnienceau Taylor, chairman of social committee.

Picture reprinted with the permission of F.D. Bluford Library archives North Carolina Agricultural and Technical State University.

Chapter 6
George Meets Ruth

I was a real shy fella, but as soon as I saw that girl, I knew I wanted to talk to that girl. I mean this chick was fine. So I kept looking at her, and for two years I looked at her. I ain't lying, for two years I looked at her! I couldn't get up enough nerve to talk to her until that one day we were going on a band trip, and she was running late. I was on the bus sitting by myself, and I looked up and she came floating down that aisle on the bus I was on. And boy, she could float. One of the guys said, "There's a seat next to George." I said, "oh boy! Here it is now."

-George Halsey

I now know why I had to go to A&T. I went to get an education, and to find love.

George and I met on a bus. This bus was rented by the Athletic Department for the band to travel to the football game. That particular day—I remember it was a Saturday—we had to play in Durham. We were both beginning our freshman year but George stayed on campus. I didn't stay on campus, so Daddy had purchased the new Buick and would drive me to school when he had time, or I had to walk or ride the city bus. When I finally got to school, I was exhausted. Prior to that day, boys were the last thing on my mind. Sure, a couple of guys had tried to date me, but I was too busy learning how to be a college student. I was joining clubs, having fun and making my way to the top as a majorette. I loved being a majorette. From the cute outfits to the dance routines, and the long hours of practice,

I loved it all! And then like a tornado, George knocked my socks off.

He was the handsomest man you could ever set your eyes on. The first time we talked, it was awkward because George never talked

a lot. O.K...he didn't talk at all! He was so handsome though, with deep dimples; and when standing, he would stand back on his legs which was so sexy.

Every time George tells of our first encounter, he says that I asked him out on the first date because he didn't talk. But I surely didn't ask him, and it may have taken a few minutes

The Majorettes; from left to right are: Lillie McNeil, Peggy Hughes, Juanita Brown, Tiyette Neal and me. Kneeling: Barbara Dodd. F.D. Bluford Library archives North Carolina Agricultural and Technical State University.

for him to do it, but eventually, he figured out something to say!

He was such a gentleman. Always so neat, polite, and fun to be around. Even in his fraternity, he was the man everyone wanted to be like. When he walked across campus, it looked like he didn't have a care in the world. Even though he was the first to go to college in his family, you could never tell when things went wrong. He was always very quiet. He never talked much, but he would give a great smile. Wow. It's been well over fifty years since we first laid eyes on each other, and I can still remember that smile. When George spoke to me, I felt like the most beautiful woman in the world. When he told a joke, I'd laugh so hard. And when he played one of his instruments, I felt butterflies in my stomach. I was the luckiest woman on campus, and everyone knew it.

Not long after our first ride on the bus, we started dating. George would carry my books and walk me home, even though he stayed on campus. When he didn't walk me, he would borrow his frat brother's car and drive me; knowing that he should've been in the library somewhere studying. No one had a car in his family (I heard that a million times when we were younger), but he never let that stop him.

Sometimes I would be coming across campus waiting for George, and I'd hear him playing "My Funny Valentine" on his saxophone. That

This is the night I became a new member of Zeta Phi Beta Sorority, Inc.

was our song. On campus, it was like our special code. Whenever he was in the band room waiting, he'd play or hum "My Funny Valentine." Every girl seemingly loved him. And because they loved him, they hated me.

They really did; but I didn't care all that much. In fact, when George decided to let it be known that I belonged to him, the Delta girls decided to blackball me from pledging in their sorority! They did everything in their power to keep me out of their little club. But, instead of fighting those little girls, I decided to join the Zetas!

Their loss.

✑ THE LADIES LOVED GEORGE! ✑

People used to ask me if George ever dated any other girls before me. I don't really know the answer to that. All I know is that I'm the only woman that counted. The ladies truly loved him. No doubt about that. One time, he told me about a girl named Delores. She called herself his girlfriend, but George didn't call her that. Then, there was the stalker girl who became homecoming queen at A&T the year I graduated. She tried so hard to steal George away from me, but it was a mission impossible. I was his Funny Valentine, his "Poonkie."

Which reminds me, George never called me Ruth. Most people don't know that. He always called me Momma or Poonkie. He got the nickname Poonkie from my family, who used to call me that as a child. And I think he called me Momma because, to him, I was the only Momma that really mattered. In speeches around the world, he would always say, "There is a difference between a mother and a Momma." Then, he would point to me and say, "That's Momma!"

To him, Ruth was not easy to say with feeling. So, he decided to call me Poonkie. I never gave him a nickname, but that one stuck with me for years. In public, I was Momma; in private, I was Poonkie:

"Poonkie, I want to take you out tonight and ride around town just to check out what's happening. You think you can get your dad's car?" George whispered.

"I don't think Dad will let me borrow his car."
"Girl, you sure know how to crush a man's dreams!?"
"Oh, no! Here we go, George. I know you want me to ask Dad."

Well, I asked him. And he said yes. I told my father that I would take good care of the car, but as soon as we got out of the house, I let George drive. It ended up being the worst night of my life.

George took me out for a nice drive around town. My father had just started to let me use the car after doing so well in my Driver's Education classes. Of course, as gullible as I was back then, I trusted George with everything. We pulled right up to the front of my house and the night was perfect. I guess George got so excited about driving me around that he turned into the driveway too hard and ended up hitting the water meter! The loud noise woke up the entire house, and the dent was hard to hide. My dad ran outside and was furious. He looked at me with those keys in my hand (by the time he came out we had switched places), and I took the blame so Dad wouldn't get angry with George. Meanwhile, George sat there with that corny looking smile, as if to say "I'm sorry, Poonkie."
I bet he was.

From that point on, whenever we went on a date, we would use his frat brother's car or we caught a cab.

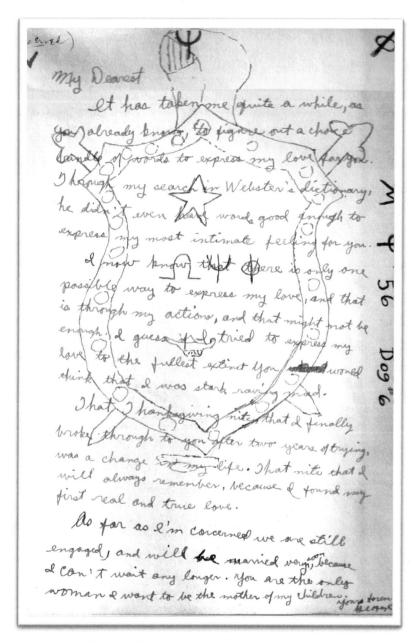

(over)

My Dearest

It has taken me quite a while, as you already know, to figure out a choice band of words to express my love for you. I through my search in Webster's dictionary, he didn't even have words good enough to express my most intimate feeling for you.

I now know that there is only one possible way to express my love, and that is through my actions, and that might not be enough. I guess if I tried to express my love to the fullest extent you would think that I was stark raving mad.

That Thanksgiving nite that I finally broke through to you after two years of trying, was a change in my life. That nite that I will always remember, because I found my first real and true love.

As far as I'm concerned we are still engaged, and will be married very soon, because I can't wait any longer. You are the only woman I want to be the mother of my children.

Yours forever
George

George wrote this in the back of my yearbook. He was letting me know that I belonged to him and that we were getting married!! And so we did get married!

The Struggling Years

Chapter 7

Mr. & Mrs. Halsey

Like every college couple, George and I had our ups and downs. We would date for a while and then we would break up. He would get on my nerves, we would get back together and then we would break up again. But, the last time we broke up, George called himself trying to date another majorette in the band. I didn't really mind though, because at the same time, a guy named Randy was trying to date me!
-Ruth Halsey

I know George saw him. Every step Randy made, George would be watching. Every move he made toward me, George would cut his eyes across the field to let us know he was paying attention. Until one day at practice, George went up to Randy and told him he couldn't take me home from band rehearsal. Of course, Randy wasn't trying to hear it, so they started a little argument right there at practice. I sat there for a little while and let them fight over me. Then, to keep everything cool, I stepped in and told George that he could bring me home.

That same night, George proposed to me. We weren't even dating at the time, but George must've realized that he was going to lose me, so he borrowed his friend's car, asked to drive me home, and during the ride he stopped at the drive-in theatre.

He said he wanted to talk.

George? Wanting to talk? I should've known he was up to

something because most days, you couldn't pay George to talk! But anyway, he pulled over that night and we started talking about why we had broken up. We went back and forth and somehow, someway, the conversation led to, "Will you marry me?" I was completely shocked! So shocked, I thought he was kidding. But George insisted. I'll never forget it. He said:

"You belong to me, and nobody else is going to have you. I want you to be my wife."

Then he reached in his pocket, and put his fraternity pin on me. The first thing I said was ...

"No!"

"No? What do you mean no?"

"I can't marry you, George! What will my mom say?"

"She'll be fine with it. It'll be fine."

"George, you know my Mama won't approve!" I insisted.

"I know, I know, but I want to marry you! We can ask Peggy and Mack to take us to Bennettsville, where they married! We can do it and nobody will have to know!"

I guess I consented because on the first of December, we eloped. I still didn't believe him when he said it, but George went downtown to get the license and asked my girlfriend, Peggy and her new husband Mack, if they would be witnesses. They, too, had snuck away to get married so we got our instructions from them.

⌒ I PRONOUNCE YOU "HUSBAND AND WIFE." ⌒

The day came for us to go and get married. I didn't know what to tell my mother, so I told her I was going to early mass with Peggy. Peggy was a Catholic, and that was the easiest way for me to get out the house, so I lied to my Mama, and we got on the road with Peggy and Mack. *Destination: Bennettsville, South Carolina*—it was about two and half hours away. We left Sunday morning and rushed back that same night. Exams were the next morning and we still had to study!

The wedding day was just like any old regular day. I remember the probate who married us— his name was Judge Newton. Other than that, I don't remember any little details, except that it took a very long time to get there. When I finally got to the courthouse, I had to go to the bathroom!

Of course, just my luck, I couldn't find a bathroom anywhere in sight. The judge was waiting. George was rushing. Peggy and Mack were calling my name. So you know what I did? I held it the entire time while we were in the probate's office. I don't remember saying "I do," I barely remember signing the paperwork. If he kissed the bride, I don't know. All I know is, I had to pee!

So the minute we finished, I went and found me a bathroom. From there, we got in the car and rode back to Greensboro. I headed home, nervous as all get-up. I didn't know how to handle the fact that I had gone out—without my mother's permission—and gotten married, but I had to go home because I had to study. George went back to campus because he, too, had an exam to study for. He kissed me "goodnight" and the next few weeks were business-as-usual.

Nobody knew but me, George, Peggy and Mack, so throughout the day, I would whisper to myself, "I'm married! I'm married." But I couldn't enjoy the moment because I couldn't tell anybody!

It was about three weeks after I got married that I broke the silence and told Roy that I had eloped. Roy was not just my little brother, he was my best friend, so I couldn't keep it from him much longer. The first thing he said when I told him was...

"Fool! You lying!"

I told him I was serious—we were married, but I couldn't tell anybody because I knew Mama would get mad.

You know what happened next.

Roy went and told one sister, and one sister told another, and soon enough, word had spread throughout the house like wildfire! By the time Mama found out, she was furious. She was first mad that I got married; then she was mad that I didn't tell her first! She was just mad. I can hear her now...

"So what are you talking about being married?"
"Mama, I am married."
"What do you mean?" she said as she clinched her teeth together.
"I mean, we went to Bennettsville and got married. Peggy and Mack took us, and –"
"Bennettsville huh?"
"Yes Ma'am, Bennettsville. And I know –"
"Well," she interrupted. "You don't know what you are doing. I swear he's going to get you pregnant. That boy quit you and you still went ahead and got married...like this? You're only 20 years old, Ruth Helen! I ought to take you back and have it annulled."

Oh yea, she was definitely upset with me. But she never forced me to go back and change anything. They were disappointed, but in time they accepted it as something they couldn't change and moved on.

∽— I GUESS IT WAS A HONEYMOON... —∽

George took me to meet his family for the first time a few weeks after my family found out. I guess it was our little honeymoon, (if that's what you want to call it), but it wasn't anything fancy. We went to Wilmington for a few days, and while we were there, Uncle James took us to dinner at the Shriner's Club. It was a regular-looking restaurant, but it was a really nice gesture. He called himself taking us out to celebrate. So, anyway, after I told Mama that we had eloped, she swore up and down that I would get pregnant. I insisted that I wouldn't. But she would continue speaking like I wasn't even talking:

"Ruth Helen, there's no way in the world you're going to be able to stop it. You're going to get pregnant."
And I would say, "No Mama, I ain't getting pregnant. Besides, George told me he was sterile."

Yes! That's what he told me. George said I didn't have to worry about a thing because he was sterile, therefore I couldn't get pregnant.

Well, on the way back from Wilmington, I started getting real sick. I didn't know what morning sickness felt like to call it that, but about a week later when I went to the doctor, you know what they told me, right? Yes! I was pregnant.

Five months later, I was stepping across the field at A&T to receive my degree in Physical Education, and four months after that, I was delivering Karen Michelle on September 4.

⌐ *WELCOME KAREN MICHELLE HALSEY!* ⌐

Having Karen was a once in a lifetime deal, and I do mean once-in-a-lifetime. When I had Karen, I had a dry birth, which meant my water didn't break. She laughs when I tell the story, but I mean it when I say, "My water never broke." She says it had to have broken at some point, but all I know is that it hurt, it hurt, it hurt! Giving birth was the craziest pain I ever felt in my life! So much so, that after I had Karen, I told George, "the only way we will have another baby is if you have it!" And I meant it.

Karen at 2 years of age. It's here were George began calling her "Punkin" for short.

Karen was a tough little something. After what seemed like hours of me screaming and carrying on, they knocked me out and I woke up to this pretty Black baby. I remember the nurses—there were a lot of them, with my mother and sister, hanging around my bed, placing this pretty baby up in my face. All of them were pointing, "Look at your new baby! How pretty." The first question I had was, "What is it?" –I didn't even know if it was a boy or a girl! So they told me, "Oh it's a little girl! She's so pretty!"

And they were right. Karen was such a pretty baby. I could hardly believe I had even had a baby because after the doctor injected me, I went out completely. When I finally realized where I was, I was in another room and very sore.

George was in Bronx, New York when Karen was born. Once he got the call that she was here, he started singing and swirling around on the sidewalk, "I've got a girl! I've got a girl, my wife just had a girl!" I just can't imagine George with his shy self, singing in the street! But he did. I think he secretly wanted a boy (even though he never said it) because he taught our daughter everything he would have taught his son.

They became best friends. Every Saturday morning she would wake up early to join him in our bedroom for Saturday morning cartoons. He loved them, especially the cartoon Under Dog. I would hear them singing the opening song..."Look...up in the sky, is it a bird?, is it a plane?, no it's UNDER DOG!!!" Then they would burst into laughter and settle in. He would tell her stories of his childhood, "The Goldfish Story" was her favorite. She would laugh each time as if she had heard it for the first time. They would then have the pillow fight that I would promptly interrupt. I didn't want them tearing up my pillows! Sometimes he acted just like he was a child! She liked cars, just like he did. She had more toy cars and trucks than baby dolls. She followed him around like a shadow. I couldn't believe he had her driving and changing gears when she was 6 years old.

Shortly after that he introduced her to his gun collection, yes, I said gun collection. He taught her gun safety, how to clean it and then how to shoot it! I saw her once with a double barrel shotgun showing no signs of fear. She pulled the trigger, both barrels went off, it knocked her to the ground and she got up laughing!

Then he started buying dogs (plural). He wanted cats too, but I was afraid of cats, so that wasn't an option. But he made up for it with dogs. House dogs, hunting dogs, dogs for protection. You name it; we had it. You would see George, Karen and the dogs. If they weren't taking care of the dogs we had, he was out looking for new ones. I had to put my foot down about the number of dogs we would have at one time. He thought he would have a hunting partner with Karen, but she was too soft hearted to kill anything, so they would pretend to go hunting. Instead of shooting animals, they would lay in the tall grass, eat pound cake (their favorite) and talk of the places they would go and the things they would do. He would eventually just set up some cans and they would have target practice. They were two peas in a pod. If he loved it, she loved it.

Chapter 8
Making Ends Meet

"I used to read those signs on some of those doors that said EQUAL OPPORTUNITY EMPLOYER. But when you go in there to try to get the job, you stay right where you started—at the end of the line."
-George Halsey

We got married, I got my degree, we had a baby, and then... it got worse. You know they always say it gets worse before it gets better, but for me and George, it seemed like better was moving in slow motion. For a long time, it felt like the good days were so far away from us. The first ten years of our marriage, we struggled to make ends meet. It was really hard, as a Black young couple, to move up in the world. It wasn't that George was lazy or that I was unmotivated. I did all I could to help out as a teacher and a new mother, but when we first got married, we couldn't even live together. George went North to find a good paying job, and I stayed home with my mother to teach. I think he had every job you could think of! Still, it seemed like we weren't making it.

First, George landed a job folding boxes in the Mattress Factory. He would tease while demonstrating, "You get to this side, fold this way, turn this way and then fold it this other way. It takes a whole lot of education to fold boxes!" He worked that job for a while until one day his boss came over and said something he didn't like and, well, George laid him out on the mattress. Needless to say, that was the end of that job.

Then he got a job at a big corporation. He would often say, "I started at the top!" He started at the top alright! He had to sweep those steps from the 15th floor down to the bottom. Then George's brother-in-law encouraged him to apply to the police force. During the interview, they told him he was a half an inch too short. George said that he grew half an inch right on the spot and they hired him! He was a policeman for about seven years. They nicknamed him the little bitty police officer

George as a police officer on Market Street.

and started him out walking "The Beat" on Market Street.

Now, for those who don't know, when a police officer walked "the beat," that pretty much meant you were patrolling on foot. Market Street was on the Black side of town. You found a little good, but there was a whole lot of bad. It definitely wasn't a good area for a young lady to be out at night by herself. People challenged him because he was so short, but after laying a few of them out, he gained a lot of respect.

Everything wasn't so great on the force. In fact, the bad ended up outweighing the good. During George's time as a policeman, Greensboro was one of the most racist places in the South. A lot was going on with Race Riots in full swing. Boycotts were happening everywhere and whites and blacks were so divided, we didn't bother to talk to anyone that wasn't Black. We kept our distance and minded our business.

One day, while George was working on the force, a riot broke out on campus. It was so serious that a student was killed. George came home with blood all over his uniform. I don't know what happened exactly because George never completely told us (I guess he was trying to protect us). He was just at the wrong place at the wrong time. He was right in the middle of it, and he had to fight off whoever was in his face. He slowly walked in the house after his shift and I saw all this blood. I'll never forget it. We were shaken up. We hugged him and George was just George: trying to calm us down and letting us know he was okay. But suffice is to say, not many months after that, George turned in his uniform and ended his career as a cop.

It wasn't just because of the violence that he turned in his uniform though. At the time, George was never able to climb the ladder of success. In fact, every time a promotion came his way, they would never give it to him. The first excuse was that he wasn't qualified. He hadn't finished his degree. So that excuse worked for a while, but when George finished his studies at A&T, they came up with some other reason to keep him from going any higher in his career. And if you know George, you know: he was never satisfied with staying on the same level. He was too big a thinker to be satisfied and complacent in the level he was in. I think that's why the Amway business, later on, really fit us as a couple. We were both competitive. We both loved challenges and neither one of us settled for what someone said we couldn't attain. If someone else could do it, we could, too!

So after being caught in a holding pattern with the police force,

George decided to dabble in a few more jobs. At one point, he tried to sell some Steward McGuire shoes; but the man didn't talk so that didn't work out too well. Then, he was hired by Nationwide as a claims adjusters. As an insurance agent, he was given a company car and he carried his attaché case with pride and dignity. I'll never forget that car. George had a burgundy Chevrolet Impala. He loved it because his family never had a car to call their own. He drove it like it was one of the fanciest cars you'd ever laid your eyes on. He was a true businessman at this point in his life—in fact, he was one of the first black claims adjusters for Nationwide. When George went to conferences for Nationwide, most times he'd be the only Black representative standing out in front of a lot of white people. Now if you ask me, God was preparing him all along for the next chapter in his life. He was always neat. He wore a nice suit and necktie every day. He believed in showing up to work on time, and he never let anyone talk him out of an opportunity.

ꝏ— HE PROMISED ME A HOUSE! —ꝏ

"One day, Momma and I were in the band room, and I started talking to her. I said, "If you marry me, you'll never have to work. I'll put you up in a big house, with fine cars, and mink coats and diamond rings. And yes fellas, that's what we tell them when we're courting. But when you get married, they call it lying!

So we got married and I got me one room; it was one room up in a ladies attic. Momma was upset because she had never forgotten the promise I made her. So I spent some more money and got us a four room apartment. I was so excited I couldn't stand it. I thought I was moving up in the world, but she was still mad.

"Where's the big house?" She'd ask me. And she kept bugging me about it. Until one day, I finally got really adventurous and I went out and got me a five-room house; it was a brand new house. I was so turned on I couldn't stand it, boy, and I guess we stayed in that house for about

three years. And then one day we were sitting there in the living room and she said,
    "George, you know, I don't want a big house."
    And I said, "I know what you mean. I don't either."
    She said, "yea, because I'll just work myself to death trying to keep it clean."
    I said, "I know what you mean." Then I said, "And I don't like Cadillacs either. That big old car, burning all that gas."

    And she said, "Yea and you know what? I don't like diamond rings either. Somebody can come along and cut your finger off and all that, you know?"
    What happened that day is what is happening to many people right now. We were reducing our dreams down to our income. We wanted to live in a big home, but we were never taught to dream. But one good thing about Momma is that she would always push me to do more. She used to tell me, "if you can dream it, you can do it."

-George Halsey

By this point, we had been on a financial roller coaster for about ten years, but things were slowly starting to level out. For a little over a decade, Karen had been an only child and I told you, my mind was made up: I wasn't pushing out another one. But George wanted another baby. He wanted a boy and I wanted a girl. So we decided to adopt. Now, most people who know us today, have no clue about our decision to adopt John. And needless to say, the process was one of the most difficult things we had ever done. The agency wanted us to do so much before releasing John to us—background checks, references, income reports, this file and that application; the entire process took about a year before we got him. We had only seen pictures of him. (no home visits) But the day we met John was a memorable one.

July 27, 1969. John was 5 years old when his caseworker called us and told us to meet him at the park. Everybody was happy except

Karen. The caseworker had explained to John that they were only going to the park to play. She told us that we were going to the park to watch him play. Well, by the time the day ended, John was in our car, we were driving him back to our house, and he was crying all the way, "I want Miss Louise!"

You heard right. The caseworker told us to take him home that day, and John had no clue who we were. To him, we were two people kidnapping him from his caregiver, Miss Louise. That boy cried and cried and cried. For weeks, he would ask for Miss Louise.

"I want Miss Louise!"
"Can you call Miss Louise?"

Early on, John even tried to run away and find this white lady by the name of Miss Louise! I don't know who was to blame for all this, but I don't think the folks in the Adoption Agency took enough time to allow our son to transition. He was scared out of his mind and Karen was jealous. She couldn't stand another child coming into the family and taking attention away from her. She'll tell you today, when John first came in our home, they were always going at it. Even after years of their growing up together, John and Karen didn't get along very well. Eventually, both of them grew out of it, but the new addition to our family made our lives all the more interesting. Having a child for whom you never had to change diapers, was different. Hearing him call me "mom" was a great thing, but it took some time getting used to. And John, for the great majority of his childhood, was a really good kid. Everybody thought he was going to become a preacher because in elementary through middle school, John was the church-going, positive boy who didn't really get in much trouble. But that quickly turned sour in high school, when John began to get into things that he had no business getting into.

∾ *WHAT I LEARNED FROM JOHN* ∾

Every relationship teaches you a lesson about life. And what I've learned from John is that parents need to give love, give love, give love—no matter how their children act out. John and Karen were both raised in a household full of love. We didn't show partiality toward either of them, although Karen might say otherwise—we tried our very best to bring them up in a good home and nurture them the best way we could. But the fact of the matter is, some children will do what they want to do. It wasn't my fault that one child turned out one way and another child turned out another way. I tried to be the best mother I could be, and that was what sustained me during those times when John began stealing from us, or getting involved with drugs. Like I said, he wasn't a bad kid--never has been--but negative influences can turn a good kid bad, any day.

What I'm most grateful for about John is that he respects us, he loves us, and he calls us from time to time. He's doing much better now because he's always known that we love him. And I do love him.

But anyway, I said all of that to say, George and I were able to adopt because we were moving up in the world. We were climbing up the ladder from room, to an apartment, to home ownership. We actually bought a bigger house every seven years. For Black folks, anywhere in the US, we were doing pretty good. During this time, when we lived in the apartment, just for a little while, we shared our apartment of four rooms and a bath with the now world-known Jesse and Jackie Jackson. George met Jesse at A&T State University. They were Omega frat brothers and friends. Friends to the point that when Jesse and his wife needed a place to stay, they stayed with us in our apartment, slept on our couch and I had the privilege of naming their first child, "Santita." We have great respect for the Jackson family.

~ THE TRUTH WAS... ~

My job was stable. I was a Physical Education teacher, coaching basketball and assisting all of the other sports. I also headed up a dance troop called the Pirateers of Page High School. George, on the other hand, was bringing in steady income as a claims adjuster. So I thought we were doing it big.

Me coaching the Page Girls Basketball Team.

In reality, we were living paycheck to paycheck. We rarely paid our bills off because we never could afford that. We didn't have money saved up or a good retirement package, but it didn't bother us because we also were able to enjoy a few "toys" of our own.

Being married to a dreamer with no money can be a challenge. He once bought 2 motorcycles, one for Karen and one for himself that neither of them could ride! He put the cycles in our den in front of the television and they would watch T.V. sitting on the motorcycles that they didn't know how to ride. I'm laughing to myself thinking of when "Gunsmoke" came on T.V., they would jump off the bikes, get on opposite sides of the room, pretend they had guns and were having a standoff. When it came time to shoot, George would fall to the floor, Karen always won, they'd get back on the bikes and look at the show. By spring, I made them get those bikes out of our house.

The first camper we had, George pretended he was just displaying it for the company he worked for. After about 2 weeks of "displaying" it, he suggested we take it on a trip. I told him I wasn't traveling in something that didn't belong to us. It was then that he told us he had bought it! That was how we started camping. We didn't know anyone that camped, we learned as we went along and believe me I wasn't happy about it initially, but we kept going. Most times, we would take a lot of the kids in the neighborhood so they could have the experience too. In those days, Blacks didn't camp at all so we were going to places that didn't always welcome us.

That didn't stop George. With his map, he would just look until he found one that would. I married a man that wouldn't stop when he ran into a wall. He would back up, try another direction until he got what he wanted! We traveled the entire east coast of North America this way, from Quebec, Canada to Key West Florida. Every summer we would pick a location on the map, and go. We would take the rest of the year to pay for the trip we just had so we could plan another one the next summer.

By 1973, I was driving a brand new Lincoln Mach 3 and George had moved us into a 4,000 square foot home. Yes, I got my five-bedroom home. George likes to tell the story that when we moved into this home, a week into it, I was already dreaming about the next one! We still had boxes in the living room, but I was saying, "So George, when we get our next house..." That's how I was. Even in the home we lived in on Highberry, we couldn't afford it (to be honest) but we thought we could. In fact, we applied for a second mortgage on top of the mortgage we were pre-approved for! But in our minds, this was far better than what our parents had done. So we were proud of our accomplishments. We were proud of where we had come from and where God had blessed us to see.

Like George, I was never content. I was always reaching for something bigger and better. I just didn't know where bigger and better was or how to get it. We had two children now, a truckload of bills, and we were living above our means.

That's when a young white couple came into our lives. Because of them, our lives changed forever. Their names were Mark and Carolyn Williams.

Chapter 9
The Greatest Decision We Ever Made

Every morning a Giselle awakens. And it knows that it must run faster than the lion or it will be eaten. Every morning in Africa, a lion awakens, and it knows that it must run faster than the Giselle or it will starve. So it doesn't matter if you are a Giselle or a lion, when the sun comes up, you better be running. I'll see you at the top!
-George Halsey

It always pays to do good by people. When your heart is full of love, you can't help but to give. And when you have a giving spirit, even if you don't have a lot of money, you can still make a difference in people's lives by being considerate, compassionate, and concerned. If anyone knew how to do this well, it was George. George was always doing good things for people, even if those same people weren't doing good things for him. He was the generous kind of guy who would make sure everyone was benefiting, or else he wouldn't accept a gift for himself alone.

Our journey with Amway began not because we had the inside scoop on this successful company. We found Amway because George was busy doing a good deed for a man named Mr. Bennett. Mr. Bennett introduced George to another man whose name was Mark Williams. The story is very interesting, so keep up with me. Mr. Bennett and George worked together at the same insurance company. George tells it better than I do, so I'll include his recap. It's a speech he has told all around the world. Every time we went out to speak, we would tell thousands of listeners how we stumbled upon the greatest business decision we would ever make:

This is our sponsor, Mark Williams and his wife.

While I was working on the job, there was a guy in my office who was an agent. He was kind of new and I would give him prospects. So he got really excited about that because nobody was helping this guy out. It wasn't a big deal to me. I wanted him to do well, so I would bring him new prospects every so often. Until one day he said, "George you know what I'm going to do? I'm going to turn you on to something." Now all the while, I had been telling the guys at my job that I wanted to sell my motor home. It was an old motor home-- no air conditioner, it needed a fresh paint job, and I wanted to get rid of it-- so Mr. Bennett set up a little game between me and my soon-to-be sponsor. He planned to send Mark over to my house to look at my motor home, or so I thought; and in the process, Mark was going to show me "The Plan." I was in the middle of it trying to sell my motor home, and so, all of us wanted something from the other person. At first, Mr. Bennett told Mark to come by my house, but Mark wouldn't come because someone told him that black folks couldn't do this business; so he didn't bother to call.

A few days later, Bennett walked over to me and asked, "Did Mark ever call you?" I told him no. Then Bennett says, "Well let me call him again."

And he called him again. This time, Mark answered the phone and contacted me to make an appointment to meet at the house. Now… suppose he hadn't called me back? Suppose Bennett did not check in with Mark? I would be on my way to work on Monday!

So Mark finally calls and says, "Mr. Halsey, I'm expanding my business in your area and we are looking for a few sharp people that we would like to involve. And Mr. Bennett told me about you."

I said, "Well that sounds very nice."

Then I thought, maybe if I can get him to come over to the house, then he would buy the motor home and I'll listen to what he has to say and be done with the whole deal. Sure enough, Mark came over that night and before I could show him the motor home, he showed me the plan. And as soon as he showed me the plan, I got excited! I knew that was it. After he finished his presentation, Momma was sitting there with her jaws poked out, mad. Mark said, "I want you to listen to these tapes, read this literature," and that's exactly what I did. I went to work the next morning, and the first thing I said when I opened the office door was. "Boyyyyyy! You can make a lotttt of money!"

After my co-workers finished laughing at me, I went home and quit from the business on the very first day I got in.

I called Mark and said, "I don't think I'm going to do it." He brought another tape over to my house and then I got fired up again.

Went back to the office the next day, they were still laughing at me. So I figured "I shouldn't get in this." Got home, called Mark and said, "I can't do this. It won't work." Mark lived about sixteen miles away. He came over and sat in my kitchen and looked me right in the eye and said…

"Well George, I didn't think you could do it anyway."

That was the last thing he should've said. I don't think he really knew what he had said to me. Here it was: a 21-year-old white guy sitting in my kitchen in front of my wife, telling me that I couldn't do it? Well boy, he sure got me fired up. I walked away from that table thinking, "I'll show you buddy." I told Mark, "You tell me how to do it, and I'm going to do everything you say for one year, and if it doesn't work, then it's your fault."

And he said in response, "Well the first thing we have to do is have a meeting. Mark helped me to set it up and I had my first meeting. Whatever Mark said do, I did. If he coughed, I coughed, I was determined to follow his instructions exactly. The first meeting, a few people came— nobody got in. The second meeting, a few more people came— nobody got in. The third time, I went to a guy's house, read him the plan off of a note card. He got excited and got in!

This is the motor home we owned before we were in the business. It didn't have an air conditioner, so we used to stand next to the window to get air. Our sponsor, Mark, said he wanted to buy it, but he really wanted to show us the plan! That's how he got us into the business. This motor home helped us haul our products.

This is what George told the world as we traveled to speak for different organizations. But let me pause and clarify something. George used to always say I was mad. I wasn't really mad (I probably looked mad), but I had reasons to be suspicious. Mark Williams was a 21-year old white guy! We were black and he was white. Some people say they don't see color, but as dark as we were, there was just no way you couldn't see it.

So here this guy is saying to us that he's going to show us how to make money. But from his appearance, he didn't look like he had much money himself. Our car was better than his, from the looks of it our clothes were nicer too, and he was a lot younger than we were so I wasn't really buying it. George got excited but I didn't. I didn't know what he was talking about. I had never heard of Amway before. At least George had seen the shoe spray. But I had never even heard of the name nor seen the products. So here I am: listening to this guy talk about a business so we could make some money. George wanted about 400 extra dollars and I just wanted Mark to get out of my house!

But like the courteous woman I am, I waited until they were done with their first meeting. Mark gave him a book that night called The Magic of Thinking Big by David J. Schwartz. He told George, "Whatever you do, don't read beyond the first chapter because you won't be able to handle it. Just read one chapter for now." So of course, George stayed up all night and read the entire book! He got so excited that he went and told everybody that he was going to be rich. And I do mean everybody. Everything Mark said to do, George did it. We made the product demo exactly the way his wife made hers.

Now the interesting thing is, George was not a public speaker. Especially when he first started out, he was always so scared to talk in public that he practiced with our dog before showing it to anyone else. "Showing the plan" was Amway's way of saying that we were introducing the business to those who might be interested in joining the Amway family. You couldn't show the plan (back when we started) without a blackboard, easel, eraser, and some chalk. Well, George would get so nervous showing the plan that chalk would be sprinkled all over the place. There was chalk dust everywhere that first day he practiced. He was so excited, he didn't know what to do. So he took a day off of work and learned everything in a day. By the time I got home from teaching, he had me look at the plan and after I listened to him, it sounded like he was ready to do what he needed to do.

✑— HARDSHIPS! —✑

When we first started going, it really wasn't hard. People were getting in, we had a house full. The hard part--we would have appointments with people in town and out of town. We had worked all day on our jobs, and at night we would do meetings. I remember one time we went to Goldsboro to show the plan. It was raining. We could hardly see. When we got there, the people didn't even open the door! We even saw them peeping from the window, but they didn't answer the door.

Another time, George made an appointment in Delaware to show the plan for a couple, and when he got up there, the guy opened the door, found out it was him and said, "I thought you were just kidding." Another time he drove from Greensboro to Jacksonville, FL only for them to say that they weren't interested. That's when he learned that people had to want it more for themselves than he wanted it for them.

But anyway, back to George:

We began having meetings in my basement. The meetings began very small but eventually, I was backed up against the room drawing circles. It got to be so much that I had to separate the new people from those who were already in the business. People were walking around saying "I want to get in! I want to get in! What do I need to do?" And I'd call Mark up and ask "What do they need to do?" And Mark would say, "Well, you need to have another meeting." That was his response no matter how many times I asked the question. But it was getting wild boy, and eventually we couldn't keep up with them. That's when Momma and I sat down to figure out what to do. We started training. We started training the teachers. If it was warm and breathing, I'd show them the plan. And if you could follow instructions, I'd teach you so that you could train others. Why? Because I had a point to prove. I had set that goal for the end of the month, and we worked it hard. I would always tell them, this business is simple. It isn't easy, but if you've been in the businesslong enough, you know everything you need to know to go Diamond.

At the same time, I would say: be careful of people who will try to steal your dream. We call them "dream thieves." They look intelligent. They sound really smart. And they can come up with some theory about why it won't work. As a matter of fact, I think these dream thieves have conventions. They all say the same thing don't they? Some of them will get kits, get in your business and steal your dream. I mean, sometimes the ones who are closest to you will try to steal it. Momma tried to steal mine as soon as we got in! She'd say, "I'm not going to do that." And when my first PV check came in, it was $3.91. She laughed and said, "Boy, you ain't going to get rich doing that!" I got my second check. It was $126.00. Momma would look at me and say, "You better quit." Then if that wasn't enough pressure, she'd put my daughter on me. And Karen would come downstairs and say, "Momma don't want you to be in the Amway business." Karen told me it embarrassed her around her friends. But you know what I told her? I told her, tell your friends it embarrasses me to be broke.

So I kept on going. The third month in the business, the check was $816.00. By the fourth month, we had cleared over $2000.00 that month!

Now suppose I had listened to her? If I had, she would still be teaching and coaching basketball. She would not have been in Australia last September. We would not have been able to live our dream.[1]

I have no problem saying it: George was right. It took work and prayer to help us, but in less than two to three years, we were making super money! At one point I was missing payday from my full time job. Money was coming in so quickly, we didn't know what we were making. We really didn't. We hadn't experienced anything like this before so everything was new to us. I'd like to pretend that we knew exactly what we were doing but the most accurate way to describe it is that we had "blind faith."

At that time, we weren't in a spirit-filled church. George didn't even like the church I went to because he's such a private person. So we couldn't claim any part of the success God brought to us—and He brought it to us quickly. Doors were opening and people were hearing.

We just kept putting one foot in front of the other. One day, my feet led me straight out of the job in which I was working. And I'll tell you what...I haven't looked back since.

The
Successful
Years

Chapter 10
The Day I left My Job...

The struggles my mom and dad experienced as a young couple helped them to become strong. Success has a lot of different meanings to a lot of different people, but what they both really wanted was freedom. Dad was fighting for freedom. Mom was fighting for freedom. They were free from traditional slavery, but my Daddy always told me, "People are still "slaves" today; they're just enslaved to their jobs. On Sunday, that chain gets tighter, and the 'Massah' pulls you back in little by little. Before you know it, you have to go back to the plantation and get back to work."

-Karen Halsey

In the Amway business, there are various levels you can achieve. The higher you go, the more money you make. When George and I began to climb the ladder of success, the levels were called Silver Producer, Gold Direct, Profit Sharing Direct, Pearl Direct, Emerald Direct, Diamond Direct, Double Diamond Direct, Triple Diamond Direct, Crown and Crown Ambassador. I won't bore you with the details of how you arrive at different levels, but if you are interested in learning more about Amway, I'd be glad to have a meeting with you!!

It took us four months to qualify as Silver Producers. We worked so hard and we had so many meetings. I can't tell you the thousands of people we met in such a short period of time. The purpose of the meeting was to establish a network of people who were committed to the very things we were committed to. We wanted to show our people the way to become independent business owners. We ended up bringing in people from all nationalities and ethnic backgrounds, but our ultimate goal was to teach Black people and empower them to become leaders. We figured that once we taught a leader, they would go on and teach others. The people in our business knew the product, how to present "The Plan" and they knew why they were doing it: to achieve their personal dreams and to help others evolve their business in order to achieve their dreams. We would say things like, "Each one, Teach one." That was our motto because relationships were important.

When the meetings were over, we were moving the product. Boy, everybody in our family had some Amway product in their house. Why? Because Amway has everything! From soap to socks to coffee to vitamins to cologne to fruit bars to popcorn to candles, air freshener, cleaning products, makeup, jewelry, light bulbs, batteries, kitchen appliances, disposable containers, trash bags, handbags, all kinds of bags! You name it, we got it! I was the product queen. My area was volume, product, and record keeping. All of it went toward increasing our product volume.

George's expertise was in theory, structure and keeping people's attention with the meetings he'd have. I was much more serious. He was much more comical. We both were friendly but everyone really, really loved George's personality. It was a family business. While one of us was taking the orders over the phone, Karen would drive the motor coach down to Summerfield to pick up tapes, books, and boards. John would help stack the tapes. Sometimes, we had almost 500 tapes in the motor coach that we'd drive back to the house. Then we had the kits, which we had to distribute to our groups who agreed to "get in." And then there was the product orders and the shipment of those orders, which we made not just for ourselves, but for others who were trying to qualify to a certain level. Some weeks, we would be on the phone up until midnight trying to help other people achieve their goal. Because we could place large orders, people would flock to our home, get the individual product they needed, and get back on the phones to see how many points they had accumulated.

In the beginning, we did everything we thought to do to get those points. We made list after list of family, friends, and co-workers. We talked to strangers and asked everyone we knew if they wanted us to come over and host a meeting. One time, I told George to sell socks to everyone. I figured if he failed at selling shoes, maybe he would do better selling socks. We sold them to his uncles, his dad, his granddad –everyone had them some Amway socks. If you had feet, we sold it to you. And for the ladies, we would sell lipstick and stockings (both were too light for Black people but we sold it anyway). Why? Because the more products you moved, the more points you received. It was a lot of work but it sure did pay off! Very quickly, I began to make more money in the business than I was making as a teacher. My income had nearly doubled in such a short amount of time. So I decided to stay on the job for two years (George would always encourage people not to quit their job, but to work at their own pace) and then, the day finally came for me to walk away.

GOODBYE JOB...HELLO JOY!

Before that day came, our days never ended. We would wake up around 6 a.m. I would get the kids up and get them ready for school. George would get up, put on his suit, necktie, and grab his attaché case. I would put on my gym clothes (usually a wind jacket and some swishy pants) with my whistle and be on our way to work. I don't ever remember cooking breakfast. I know the kids ate, but the first time I remember enjoying breakfast, it was after we had enough money to hire a personal housekeeper!

Anyway, George and I wouldn't really talk throughout the day because at that time, cell phones weren't around, and we just waited until we got home to catch up with each other. During my lunch break, I would lay out on the bench and take a nap while others were eating lunch. I did that just about every day because once I got home, we were planning to go out and show "The Plan."

We'd get home around 4:00PM. I'd put on some franks and beans, or whatever I could cook that was quick. We never ate steak. We couldn't afford steak. So most days, we had chicken or pork chops, and when I wanted to spend a little more for George, I'd make him his favorite: cube steak, peas and rice—with gravy on top. Then, after dinner, we would get dressed—George always wore a dark suit, black or gray, but never brown because he used to say that brown pulls you down. He'd have on a crisp white shirt, a tie (usually a red tie), and a red pen. Why red? Because red is most appealing to the eye. Red made you curious. And how could I forget his sweet shot. George had it with him for every meeting! We'd get the car ready, say goodnight to our children, and we would be out the door.

Early one morning, I was sitting in my kitchen writing and adding up orders to call in to the company. I had on my famous purple robe and I was probably smoking a cigarette (I was so nervous). I called my mother and said, "Mama! We're going to be rich."

Like any mother, she calmed me down and said, "honey, just calm down and tell me what you mean." I decided to go to her house because I needed something to do to work off my nerves. The business had become so huge that our family couldn't manage it all. I needed assistance and secretaries to help me out; and it still was coming in quicker than I could control. So, here I am, driving on a random street, headed to my mother's house. I was thinking, "We are going to be rich! We are going to be rich!"

All of a sudden, I went into something like a trance. I can't describe it. I don't know what happened to me. But I'm sure you've heard people say that they had an out-of-body experience. Well that's what happened. I was driving one of our luxury cars, dressed in one of the best dresses—at a certain point, I couldn't leave the house without being recognized—and I heard a voice say, "Don't say that. Don't focus on you. Focus on the people."

I heard it again.

"Don't focus on you. Focus on the people."

By the time I got to my mother's house, I was speechless. I was truly in a trance and it took about a month for me to snap back into reality. I couldn't write. I couldn't take orders. I could barely talk. I kept hearing that voice, which I know now was the Holy Spirit reminding me to "focus on the people." The moment we obeyed the voice and truly focused on the people, God took our fortune and multiplied it bigger than I could ever dream!

We went from two times a week to doing it almost every day. Work, then meetings. Work, then meetings. Finally, we got to the point that we were about to qualify as Emerald Directs. It was basketball season and I had to go to speak in Atlanta that weekend. So normally, I would start getting sick on Thursday, and then I would drag in to work on Friday so I could get out of there. I would ask Angela Watson to take over the dance classes, and I would have my co-workers, Emily Ribet and Mary Temple, to keep an eye on my P.E. classes. This particular week, I played sick again and told Mary Temple that I was leaving after lunch. I didn't report it to the office because I didn't want all those people in my business. So I left and went home, and when I got back from Atlanta, the principal was calling my house looking for me.

Monday morning, he asked me to come to his office. I reported to work as usual and I was told not to go to my classroom. Just come to the office. So I went to see Mr. Clendenin, the principal at the time, and I sat there waiting to hear what he had to say:

"Ms. Halsey," he said leaning back in his chair.
"Yes..." I replied in confidence.
"You know you've changed."
"You think so?"
"Yes, I do. If I had to evaluate you, I couldn't evaluate you the same way I once did," he said with a small smirk in his eyes.
"Well I don't know why not. I've never missed any of my classes. I

teach the same way and I'm always present," I answered sharply.

"Well, I just don't think you're doing the work that you used to do."

"Oh yes I am."

"I don't believe you are."

"Well I believe I am."

"If you were, Ms. Halsey, then I would be assured from the students and the other teachers; but I'm not. I must be honest with you."

"Well, look. You want me to leave?" I interrupted, realizing he was going to continue telling me how I wasn't doing anything right.

"Actually I think I do," he said in a very condescending way.

"Alright," I responded in less than two seconds.

"Alright?" he asked.

"Yes. You mean, you want me to leave right now?" I asked with a smile on my face.

"Yes" he said sternly.

"O.K." I sang.

I turned around, went down to the gym, opened the door to my office, and said to everyone there, "Well, I'll see y'all! I'm gone."

Emily and Mary, two white ladies in my department, were completely shocked. I left all my records and all my things for my classes and I went home.

The moment I got home, the principal started calling me to come back. The superintendent even called me to come back. I guess they thought I was going to file a complaint against the principal. What they didn't know was that his asking me to leave freed me to follow my dreams.

I didn't want to live the rest of my life as a physical education teacher. I had different goals and dreams. I wanted to make an even larger impact on my community. And Amway was the way for me to achieve that.

Miss Ribet even came over to our house and begged me to

return.

"Don't pay him any attention. He can't tell you to leave. Come on back," she said. *"You've got those classes and all that."*
To which I calmly replied, *"Well my husband doesn't want me to come back. So I won't be back."*
She wouldn't let up.
"Come on, Halsey! You know those kids want you. Come on Halsey."

But nothing she could say could change my mind. I was so happy because I had become tired of teaching. I was about to start coaching my basketball team, but with the business in full demand, it all began to weigh too heavily on me. At this point, I didn't have any more bills and I was forgetting payday. They would have to call me at one point and tell me that I had a check in the office because I was concentrating on the business money. So when I quit, it gave me much more of a desire to work the business even harder, to make sure that I didn't have to go back to work. And I never did go back. In fact, not long after I left my job, George looked up and said, "Shoot! I want to come home, too."

He worked a little while longer, and after a while, he told his boss that he was done. And he quit!

I officially left the job in 1977. George left his job in 1978, just before we qualified as Diamond Directs. And the moment we both remember like it was yesterday, was when we were sitting on the couch in the living room. He looked over at me and I looked at him, and together we both said: "We don't have a job!" We laughed and laughed until our stomachs hurt.

Chapter 11

This is Diamond

You've got people out here that care about you making it. That's what this thing is all about. And then you begin to meet these people in different places. You know, I was sitting next to a guy today, a guy named Steve, a fireman. And man, you can see it generating out of him. They are going to do it.

–George Halsey

⌒ RELATIONSHIPS, RELATIONSHIPS, RELATIONSHIPS ⌒

One thing I can say about Amway is that the company is really committed to building relationships with business partners. George was naturally friendly with everyone, so it was nothing for him to make friends. When he spoke to you, he didn't stop at friendship, he brought you into the family. We would speak around the country, and George was a genius at making people feel special. He would eat with someone in the group—most times they were complete strangers to us—and he would get to know a little about that person's life, his family, his children's names, and at night, in front of thousands of people, he would talk about this person like they were high school friends! For George, the joy of this business was tied up in the people he was able to meet and impact. In fact, if you want to know the truth, our business took off the moment we took our eyes off of ourselves and began to think about helping other people. It was the people that helped us to become successful. Without those important relationships, we would have failed from the very beginning.

◦— FORSAKE NOT SMALL BEGINNINGS —◦

I always tell my groups not to worry about beginning small. If you measure your personal success by someone else's, you'll forget the process they went through to get there. You also forget that God has a path for each of us, and if He has done it for one, He can do it for you

The beginning of the road is the most difficult. It's hard because people may laugh at you, like they did George. They will call you everything from a crazy person to a manipulator. Oh trust me, George and I have heard it all. George was rejected so many times, but somehow, he kept pushing through the negativity, and he kept on focusing on the people who were interested in the business. And soon enough, we were laughing our way straight to the bank.

The "Whootie Who's" are what we called the people we invited to come to our first meetings. They did not get in and they were always so negative. They told George stuff like, "Ain't no white man gonna show no black man how to make money." They would try to fill our hope with poison, shut down our dreams, and disqualify our faith. So George called them "doe doe birds" or something that would make his group laugh, and he kept on showing the plan. Low and behold, one day, someone did join –then another, and another, and another. Those first six couples who joined our business, becoming (at the least) Direct Distributors, made a serious impact on our lives.

The first couple we showed the plan to, we went to their house. George was so nervous that he wrote the entire plan on a 4X6 card, he literally read the entire plan from that card. When George tells this story, he said he was so nervous that he started to sweat, I mean really sweat. The sweat got so bad that it dripped into his eyes and he couldn't read the card! But instead of asking for a napkin or a handkerchief, you know what he did? He kept on talking! whatever George presented, this guy would say, "really?" George would say, "yeah man! Absolutely!"

They didn't have a clue how nervous George was. And George didn't have a clue what he was talking about. He was just excited to be connecting with someone who seemed interested in the business. When they said they wanted to do it, we acted very reserved and calm. We didn't want him to know how excited we really were. We had gotten a few "no's" before we showed them the plan.

When we got home, it was over! We started doing the happy dance and shouting, "We sponsored somebody!!!" All the while giving each other high fives. That was a good night, the night that built our belief that we could do this! This thing could work!

Then we had our second couple, whom George met at the service station on Phillips Avenue in Greensboro. Over time, we all became good friends prior to joining Amway. So, when it came time for us to make a list of people we knew, we wrote down their names. They had that fire in their eyes to do something, and do it now. So, we were invited to their house after George went to the service station one day, and dropped one of his PV checks on the ground "by accident." Of course, the man jumped down to pick it up and when he saw the amount on the check—I think it was something like $2400 (which was a lot of money back in 1975), his wife was hooked! He got so excited, he called his wife and told us to show them the plan that very night. After the first session, they got in. But here is where God's hand was in it the whole time. Not long after they got in, there was a gas crisis in Greensboro. No one could travel outside of the city because the gas stations had to ration out how much gas each family could get. But, by knowing Eugene through the business, we got all the gas we wanted. We were able to travel, not because of how much money we had, but because of the relationships we established.

Then we had our Third Directs from Winston Salem. The man was the most cooperative person we ever sponsored. He literally came to us and asked if we would please sponsor him in the business. That's how we met him. I didn't know that man from Adam's housecat. But we showed him the plan, sponsored him and he did everything we told him to do. He went Direct; then he broke Direct and became an Emerald in our business.

We then moved to our fourth in line. They are cousins of ours to whom we showed the plan and they got in very easily. The same night, he was determined to master the business. So he got up and started showing us how he could do that thing. He impressed us so much that in a few days, he was out hosting meetings himself!

Then there was our fifth couple. We met them because George was selling motor homes. He came to check out the motor homes, just like our sponsor Mark was going to do. We developed a relationship with this excited couple and one day, they invited us over their house to show them the business. He got excited and went Direct. We were not just business partners, we were friends with every person we sponsored. We wanted them to enjoy life, pursue their dream, and do better this year than they did last year. We were coaches, listeners, encouragers, helpers, supervisors and more! Whatever they needed us to be, we became what they needed.

The sixth couple, we met them camping at Kerr Lake. She and I were in different social clubs together; you know, like "Guys and Dolls" meetings and things like that. Later, she became a Zeta and we were sorority sisters. It was all uphill from there. They started camping with us regularly, and not many Black people went camping when me and George made it a hobby. We became great friends but they were very reluctant about getting into the business. In fact, the only way I got her to follow me with the business, is when I told her that I wasn't going back to my job. She told me I was crazy. I told her I didn't have to teach, and I showed her my check so that she and her husband could look at it. They looked at it and still decided not to do it. But, I didn't let up. I waited a little while and then I brought another one of my checks to their home. They decided to take another look at it. We went over and showed them the plan again. This time, they decided to do it. They got in the business, we conducted their first meeting, and in their first meeting, they invited another couple, who also got in.

Now the interesting thing is, that couple went Diamond in less than 2 years! He had a speech impediment but that didn't stop him. The first couple we showed it to went Diamond, and in that leg, (a "leg" is the terminology we use to describe an organizations team) we had Diamonds in depth! Everywhere we traveled, someone was going Direct, Pearl, Emerald and Diamond!

It was so much to take in.

Our great friends and Diamonds, Lloyd and Pam Glover.

"Two years later, we qualified as Double Diamond. In August of 1982, we qualified for Triple Diamond. We were the first Blacks to ever achieve Diamond, Double Diamond, or Triple Diamond status. There was no trail in front of us, no mentors to guide us, and no roadmap to look at. We were the trailblazers. We were the couple inspiring other couples like us to believe in their dreams. Here we were: a little black family starting our business with a $35 investment (That's what it cost for us to get in when we began). I didn't even have $35.00 to spare at the time!

Chapter 12

Dream Weekend

We have a saying...if the horse is dead, get off. If something isn't working for you, why are you still doing it? We see so many of our people doing the same things and working on the same jobs and not living out their dream. But then we look at the Amagram, and we don't see our people in it! Well, I'm going to tell you something. George and I are going to make sure more Black people are in the Amagram. It isn't impossible to do. Just do the work and always put God first. That's my belief. You don't have to know it all. Just put it in His hands. Just say, Lord bless it and He will.

-Ruth Halsey

"The Amagram" was a quarterly magazine that would go out to all of Amway's distributors. It introduced the New Directs, Rubies, Emeralds, Diamonds, and so on of the corporation. George and I were featured in that magazine a lot, but when I mentioned the "Amagram" in that speech in 1993, I was trying to rally our people to get up and do something. At this event we called "Dream Weekend," there were hundreds of people, all hoping to see something they had never seen before. Our only job was to make them see the dream. We would display the Ex Calibur, Mercedes, Jaguar, Rolls Royce's, motor homes, and pictures of our boat and private jet---we'd wear all our jewelry and bring our furs, and anything else you could imagine! Yes, we owned a twin-engine Beechcraft airplane and a cabin cruiser, which we kept docked at our second home in Hilton Head, S.C.

When we got the plane, it came as a total shock to me. George being George, walked in one day and said, "Poonkie, I was thinking...

let's get a plane." I looked at him and said, "George, a plane?" And he looked at me with that dimple on one side of his face and said, "Yes! If they make them, why can't we buy one? Think about it. We can get around a lot easier, and we can afford one, so let's get it."

I wasn't into cars but this was my Excali-bur that George bought me and his Rolls Royce. They were "black on black with red accent stripes."

This is George's boat above. Most times it sat in the driveway or at the dock in Skull Creek Marina in Hilton Head. George couldn't figure out how to dock it. He'd get frustrated and I'd laugh and he finally gave up.

This is the plane we owned. It was a Beach Craft Duke 6 passenger. George kicked the tires and I liked the curtains, so we chose this one.

Not long after that, we owned one. What I liked the most about our plane was the interior. It had six seats for our guests; and best of all, it had the nicest curtains! George knew if I was going to ride in it, I wanted it to look nice. He wasn't all that concerned about the beauty of the plane. He was kicking tires, asking about the safety and the mechanics of the plane.

I'll never forget what it was like to ride in that plane the first time. George called our pilot, Greg to schedule our flight. You could tell that the people who worked there weren't used to Black people boarding a private plane because everyone was staring at us. George was in his classic black leather suit. And I was in a casual St. John. *We were so nervous. We didn't know what we were supposed to do.* I was scared because the plane was so small. The pilot told us, "It's going to be fine. I got it." So I got on.

George and I flew to New York to have dinner and go shopping.

What was comical about our plane ride was the landing. Every time we arrived to the designated area for private planes, people would look at us very strange. I think they assumed we had leased a plane until they looked up and saw the tail of it, which read: HALSEY'S DREAM MACHINE.

Sometimes we would fly our friends in the business down to Miami or Hilton Head and then we would shoot back to Greensboro to sleep in our bed. George liked to have someone drive one of our cars down to Hilton Head for us. We'd fly over for a few days, and someone would be at the airport with our car, waiting to escort us wherever we needed to go.

George & me

But anyway, everything was there at these events to help people get out of those seats and begin to see the dream. When George and I spoke at Dream Weekend or an event of this caliber, no matter where we went, in the U.S. or abroad, they treated us like royalty. Everyone was so pleasant. We had a host to carry our luggage. They fed us all we could eat. They would even give us personal tours of the area. Anything we wanted to see or do, they made it happen.

Everyone would ask us to speak. We were a power couple. They would usually give us an hour to talk. George and I would alternate. Most of the time, I'd start off and he would finish. He would send the crowd home laughing, thinking, and believing that they could do it even better. I can't say it enough. That man was a smart man. Yes, he giggled and joked the whole time, but his comedy was always couched in some bigger purpose. I, on the other hand, was the straightforward "business" woman. I needed you to know the facts and I was never ashamed to talk about my faith. It wasn't always encouraged because people came from various walks of life, but I did it anyway. These folks needed to know that prayer works and God was behind all of our success. That's how they knew me on stage: as Momma, the straight shooter who didn't play any games.

When George spoke, he spoke directly to people's hearts. He looked straight into their eyes. Most people said he had a mischievous laugh where you'd think he was holding back a secret but then again, maybe he wasn't, but that was who George truly was. He was playful and free. He was brilliant but down-to-earth. And most of all, he cared about what people cared about. He had a way with words. He would bring up stories that would drive home the point of working hard, keeping focus, or having a plan. He knew how to motivate people. Even when people faced rejection he would tell them, "Always leave the door open." If people walked away and said, "This business is not for me," George would jokingly say:

"I can't believe it when they say that. But you know what I do to them? I just sit back in my seat and I smile and say, "well, I'm sorry you missed it." Hahahaha! Meanwhile, that dude will be sitting there wondering, "I wonder what I missed." You see, you can't let them get you. But you always leave the door open.

That was George's way of easing the pain of rejection. He understood that nobody likes rejection but everybody has to prepare for it. So he gave his listeners good information and hid it inside of his jokes. Another thing George told them to do was to develop a sense of urgency. When faced with negativity, he'd say:

Some folks that you're trying to show [the plan] to, just don't have any dreams. You're trying to put dreams in them and they don't have it in themselves. They're dead. When you're showing the plan, don't look at the dead people. Some of us will look at them and try to resurrect them. You've got to keep the momentum going. You can't slow up. You've got to put the pedal to the metal. It's not just about the technique. That's where the information is. You also need motivation and a dream. Some people think that Triple Diamonds don't get negative. But negativity can keep you broke! Boy, let me tell ya: I can always tell when somebody has gotten on Momma's nerves. I can hear the tape playing a mile away before I pull up at the house!!!

Everyone would burst into laughter, but this was one clever way for George to shift people's attention again. When he bragged about me, of course I was flattered, but there was a point to it. Sometimes, I think he was just plain ole nervous. Other times, he was trying to get people to see the importance of staying grounded, and listening to the tapes or reading the books. The materials kept you focused. And if someone didn't want to read what their up-line told them to read, he would say something like:

"Some of us will pick up a book, and that's all we'll do is pick it up. Don't just pick up one. Read the books that are suggested by your up-line. The wrong book will wipe you out. I've been in this thing for a long time. Trust me I know."

All the while people were laughing and having a good time, but George was actually teaching the fundamentals of building a successful business. George would get their attention by telling those classic stories like the Lion and the Giselle, or the Chicken and the Eagle. He knew his audience and he knew how to engage people. He didn't just come up with these ideas alone. We, too, had an upline. We had people who influenced us, and showed us the light. People like Dexter and Birdie

Yager who are now Crown Ambassadors.

The first time we met Dexter, we were invited to his house for a Pearl/Emerald reception. We had just become new Emeralds, and when we met him it was an amazing feeling. The guy was short and stocky, with very simple clothes. You wouldn't think he was really as rich as he is, until you stepped closer and saw the diamond studded Cross with the Rolex to match, which had diamonds across the entire face of the watch and the band. The rings he wore were about 7 karats on each hand, and he acted as if he had known us forever. He would put on his cute little muscle shirt, some jeans, and a cap, and keep on talking. Of course, we weren't at his home alone. There were lots of other people who had also qualified. But what stood out the most was that, AGAIN, we were the only Black couple there. Nevertheless, Dexter and Birdie were very nice. He talked with encouraging words, telling us how we had to keep the dream alive and move forward, and how impressed he was with our achievements. He told us how happy he was to have us at his home. As we walked and talked, he shared his knowledge of the business, and took all of us under his wings. As the years continued, Dexter invited us to an even larger home! Every time we met, our minds were being expanded. He would drive us around to all of these homes in the neighborhood, Show us shopping centers and complexes, and then he would stop at the stop sign and say: I own all of that.

If that wasn't enough, he would treat us to every meal, and tip the waitress no less than $50 each time we ate with him. If you were a custodian or bussing tables, it didn't matter. Dexter took the time to speak to everyone; making sure they know that they mattered. I think that's where George learned to be so out-of-the-box because Dexter would get his flashlight, and go out into the streets at 2AM to show us houses. But what was he doing? He was taking us on our own dream weekend. It wasn't difficult for us to tell people "you can do it," because every time we looked up, we saw it happening. And the technique worked every time because he knew we had it in us to make it work.

We just had to have the dream. His job was to plant the dream. Our job was to water that dream and do it.

Our mentor, leader and friend, Dexter with wife Birdie.

Dexter's wife, Birdie, is a compliment of her husband. As sweet as she could be, she would take me to her closets and the shoes, the shoes, the shoes! Her closet helped me to go back home and organize my own. Then when we went to speak for them at Free Enterprise, and they would always let the Diamonds take pictures with the guest speaker of the night.

We met a little bit of everyone: Sugar Ray Leonard, Mike Diktcha, Evander Holyfield, George Foreman, Les Brown, President Nixon, President George H.W. Bush, President Ronald Reagan, and their wives. Thanks to this exposure, our lives were changed. Our thinking was changed. I thank God that Dexter and Birdie were, are, and will always be our friends.

Our buddies Rick and Sue Lynn Setzer were no different. At the time of this writing, they are Triple Diamonds, but the sky is the limit for them. Rick is known as the "master teacher." We didn't meet Rick and Sue Lynn until we became Emeralds. When we hit that level, we could be apart of the "in crowd," so we went over to Rick's house.

Our good friends Rick and Sue Lynn.

Now all I can say is, if you want to see one fine decorated home, go over to the Setzer's house. I was immediately drawn to Sue Lynn because she was so much like me. She had such class and style. I followed her and tried to emulate her fashion sense. When I saw Sue Lynn, she was always very elegant, conservative—she looked like she could've been on the TV show Dynasty, playing the role of Mrs. Carrington. Soft spoken, poised and yet she was very funny. I took my cues from her. You couldn't get much classier than this. Before the business, they were schoolteachers from High Point living in a trailer. Now we were flying with them on the Concorde to England and swimming in their private pool!

When you flew on the Concorde, everyone knew you had made it. Tickets were something like $8,000-$10,000 to fly from New York to England. We got to England in 3 hours! That plane was so fast, George used to say that when he was on it, he could see the curvature of the Earth. He'd also say stuff like, "boy, that thing would lift straight up from the ground like a rocket ship, and take off right in the middle of the air! It lifted up and then flew away." I don't know how true all that was, but I do remember seeing Mach 1 and Mach 2 up on the walls of the plane. They served us caviar, wine, and everyone just had a good time traveling the world on this exclusive plane. *That was a good time.*

Meeting the founders of this corporation was another mind-blowing experience The first time we met Jay Van Andel and Rich De Vos, it was at our Direct's seminar. Rich De Vos spoke at the event and then afterwards, we would get to shake their hands and meet them. The experience was awesome. We were all dressed in formal attire. I was nervous and so was George. Little did we know, a few years later, we would be having dinner with them at their reserved tables in Hong Kong and Yugoslavia—everywhere! They were such down-to-earth people. They loved us. We were more than just business associates.

⌒ AIN'T NO MOUNTAIN HIGH ENOUGH! ⌒
You can have anything in this world that you want, as long as you help other people to get what they want. And you've got to take your eyes off of your self to help other people. That's a very difficult transition but that's the power. Don't worry about yourself. If you help others to make it, you'll make it.

-Ruth Halsey

After we saw the dream, nothing could stop us. George used to tell us, "Do today what others won't, so you can live tomorrow like others can't." He learned the value of working now and enjoying the fruits of one's labor later, something he often called "delayed gratification." This was our season. We had shot to the top. We were all across the globe and didn't know how we got there. One second we were in Puerto Rico (which I loved because of the stores and clothes), and then we would look up, and we were in Hong Kong, Ireland, Australia, Hawaii, Canada, London, Paris, Switzerland, Germany, The Netherlands, Belgium, Czechoslovakia, Yugoslavia, Bahamas, Acapulco, Spain, Fiji, Trinidad, and how can I forget Jamaica. *Jamaica! Jamaica! Jamaica!* It wasn't the people or the land, I just couldn't handle the goats! They would cross the street while you were driving. Everywhere I looked, I remember seeing goats. It got so bad that I didn't want to eat because everywhere we went, they had these big buffets set up. I didn't know if I was eating goat or chicken. It looked good, but I didn't want any of that stuff.

So we were traveling the world, shopping at the best stores, dining at the best restaurants. Every year, we qualified for an all expenses paid trip to Peter Island (in the British Virgin Islands) owned by Amway. When we arrived, we'd stay at the Crow's nest at the top of the mountain. We'd first fly into Miami, and then fly into St. Thomas. From there, we would take a yacht to Peter Island, and we would relax, eat, and laugh all day. Oh, by the way, the cabanas were at least $10,000 per week, so none of the menus at the restaurants had prices on them. This was the place where kings, queens, and celebrities hung out.

Not long after all of this exposure to other countries, came the magazine interviews. First came *Black Enterprise* who called and asked if they could feature our story in their magazine. We agreed. Then came *Ebony*, who wanted us in a small section they called "About us." When they got some more information about who we were and what we had accomplished, they decided to turn our story into a five-page spread. But it didn't stop there. *Jet Magazine* then called. The local newspapers wouldn't stop calling. The phone just would not stop ringing! It was madness at one point. Everywhere we went, someone either had an Amagram they wanted us to sign or an article they wanted us to autograph.

Here, Black Enterprise featured us and Amway in their magazine.
Black Enterprise (c) 1978 42012BE

Leaving home for one of their frequent out-of-town trips, George and Ruth Halsey, in matching coyote coats, pause on the staircase of their 13-room Georgian-French home (below) in Greensboro, N.C. At right is the dining room with Chinese Chippendale furnishings. The table setting is Lenox crystal and china with goldware Mrs. Halsey bought during a trip to London.

PHOTOGRAPHS BY
MONETA SLEET JR.

George and Ruth Halsey

A 'Dream Home' Is Only One Of Their Dreams That Have Come True

There's the beautiful house in Greensboro, but there are also a plane, five cars, a condominium and many other signs of their business success

NINE years ago, George Halsey was thinking of ways to earn an extra $400 a month so he could buy a new camper. He was an insurance claim adjuster and his wife, Ruth, was a schoolteacher in Greensboro, N.C., where they live, and they had a comfortable home, an old camper that was on its last leg, and little money in the bank.

Today, the Halseys own a Rolls-Royce, two Mercedes-Benzes, an Excalibur, a Corvette and a Ford Bronco.

And they have a 13-room home in Greensboro, and a boat and condominium in Hilton Head, S.C. They are part-owners of the modern, 380-room Sheraton Plaza Hotel in Columbus, Ohio, and the day-care center they partly own in Greensboro will soon become a chain. To get down to Hilton Head or to just about anywhere else they want to go, they simply drive to the local airport and board their own plane, a Beechcraft Duke, which seats a pilot, co-pilot and four passengers. A

EBONY • February, 1985

Chapter 13
The Price of Success

Halsey's Double Diamond Day in Ada

There is a high price for success. If you have money, you can buy a lot of stuff. But only God can teach you how to manage success. Many days, George and I were happy campers. On other days, life was a rollercoaster that just wouldn't stop. Like, for example, the day the company flew us to Ada, Michigan to celebrate our newest accomplishment. We hit Double Diamond status in the business, and everywhere they took us, we saw our name over every department. "Halsey's Double Diamond Day!" the banners would say. We walked into the main building on a red carpet. We had escorts and drivers. We were picked up from the airport and driven around the city in a big coach bus. That day, both Rich De Vos and Jay Van Andel were in town, so, we sat around the table in the board room and they presented us with a beautiful picture and plaque made of charcoal, which hangs in my foyer to this very day.

This is one of the first photos taken after we officially became "Double Diamonds" in Ada, MI.

That day was heavenly. It began in heaven, and it ended in... well, heaven. We were only scheduled to be in Michigan for one day. But unlike other times, my mother stopped by my house to see us off. I remember it was early in the morning, something like 7 in the morning. She had never come to see me this early before. So I asked her why she had come all the way out to where I lived to see me, and she said very calmly, "I just wanted to see you off." She smiled and I smiled, and I headed out the door.

That was the last conversation I had with her. I didn't know it, but it was almost as if she knew she wouldn't get to see me again.

And she was absolutely right.

⌐ FROM THE HIGHEST HIGH TO THE LOWEST LOW ⌐

We flew in from Ada after a day of high celebration. Our family and friends were waiting at the airport for us. We were on Amway's private corporate jet with couches, bedrooms, and recliners; laughing about how much of a great time we had had. We were showered with gifts and acknowledgements; we had the best of foods, and we were treated like royalty. The corporate jet had flown us back home, and when we arrived on the runway, we could see hundreds of people waiting for us. My mother was there as well. Everyone was there. I know that she saw the plane come in, and she saw us land. Mary told me later on that she looked up and asked, "Is that them?" pointing toward the sky. And as soon as the plane hit the ground, she collapsed.

Everyone inside went into a panic. Outside, no one knew what was going on. Someone ran out and told Karen "Big Mama is sick." Karen ran in and saw Big Mama being placed on the floor. Her cousin, Derrick, started giving her mouth-to-mouth. Meanwhile, we were outside receiving the key to the city. Karen grabbed my arm and said, "Big Mama is sick!" We stopped everything and ran inside the airport. That's when I saw her, my mother, lying on the floor. I held her. I started to shake her...

"Mama, get up, Mama...Mama!"

The paramedics arrived shortly after, checked her, and pronounced her dead on the scene.

All of my family members –my dad, my brothers and sisters, Karen –all of us were gathered around stunned, not believing what had just happened. We were just numb; shocked with disbelief.

The rollercoaster began.

I felt emotions that I had never felt before. My life was sucked out from under me. My mother had been my cheerleader. She was my encourager. She was my stabilizer. She would calm me down and keep me focused. She was the woman I looked up to in every way. I would run to her house to update her on what George and I were doing, but now, that was gone from me. I would no longer be able to do that. She was gone. In the span of 24 hours, I had moved from high to low in what seemed like minutes. I was nauseous and confused. How did this happen? Am I dreaming? George and I continued to travel after that day, but for me, it was never the same.

High again.

We continued to build our business. We were back on the road— building, teaching, running hard, driving, and doing what we do best. Then came Triple Diamond. George used to think that Triple Diamond meant that the money would triple, but it was so much more than that. Soon after, I became a member of the Amway Board of Counsels, which was a personal accomplishment of mine. But I couldn't really enjoy that moment fully because not many days later, my dad passed away. We call it a broken heart, they called it a heart attack. It was just two years after my mother's passing.

But then there was a high. We finally got the home I always wanted!

George and I on stage as "Triple Diamonds" speaking.

∽ THE HOME I ALWAYS WANTED ∽

George and I were on our way out of the state to speak in Texas. Someone in our group told us about this house that was being built in the "uppity part" of Greensboro. So we drove through and saw it. It was still in its beginning stages. As a matter of fact, I remember seeing it at night and trying to squeeze through the window just to look around. It was love at first sight. There was nothing else around it and I knew that I needed to see this house in the daylight. So we spoke to the realtor, and he told us that someone "really serious" was already looking at the house. That meant if we wanted it, we would have to put some money down before we left. We wrote him a check for $5,000 and we left for Texas.

Within a few short hours, the guy who was laying the bricks started telling people that the Halsey's had bought this big house. Word spread like wildfire, and when we got back, we were the talk of the town again! The builder placed a sign out in the front that read "SOLD." Everybody talked and some people whispered, "Who do they think they are...those Halsey's moving on this side of town?" Mind you, we were already in a very nice home. But this house was a dream house: 13-room Georgian-French home. Three levels, large hallways, spacious closets, an elevator, customized swimming pool, complete with a bathhouse and office. The master bathroom had a marble sunken tub beneath a skylight, mirrored walls and brass fixtures. It was an elegant upgrade, fit for our style and taste. I knew when we moved in, a dream home where we would retire in.

Then the rollercoaster dipped again.

George and I were determined not to let our business falter. We didn't have the business savvy to go with the money we earned, but we tried to be honest with what came in. Accountants came later. Financial advisers came later. As the money came in, people were always trying to make us an offer that we couldn't turn down. So we made good investments and we made some really bad investments. The worst of all was a car deal that someone talked us into. I don't even know the man's name or how we got this offer, but someone tricked us into believing that we could buy the car now and sell it later for a better price. Supposedly, this was one way that a lot of folks would flip their money and gain more. So we paid for it in advance. The only problem is, the car never showed up!

We don't know what happened to our money or the investment representative. Both of them disappeared and we haven't heard a thing from those people since. The lesson we learned through this was to seek out good financial counseling, and don't believe everyone that says they have a good idea.

This is our present home. I squeezed in through the balcony window to see this house and I ran back home and told George, "I have to have it." And we got it!

As we rebounded from our investment adventures, the most wonderful thing happened to us...Kislyck Mykela was born. Kissy was our first and only grandchild, born to Karen and her husband on November 29, 1985. She was the most beautiful baby we had ever seen! I thought Karen was the most beautiful baby until I saw her baby, Kissy. George beamed! He was so proud. I thought I was too young to be called Granny and George certainly didn't look like a Granddaddy, so we decided on the names Papa and Nana. We spoiled that baby! We gave her every thing she needed and every thing we thought she may

have wanted! George started calling her Booba when she was about 2 years old. He would get on stage and say my "Booba spoils me," but in reality, he spoiled his Booba. He gave her a brief case when she was around 7 or 8. A real one. It was a small burgundy leather one that she proudly carried all her papers in when we went to meetings. She would practice drawing circles (showing the plan), and even pretended to take notes during seminars.

Our children knew what broke felt like, but not Kissy. She was born at the height of our success and only experienced the best. Considering how she was raised, she has turned out to be a wonderful, hard working, well rounded individual that we are so proud of. When George would show the plan, he would pull a large amount of cash from his pocket that was rolled up with a rubber band holding it together and call it his wad. He would say, "build your business so you can become a member of the "Wad Squad!" One year on Kissy's 10th birthday, we bought her a Dooney & Bourke pocketbook with her name engraved on it complete with a wad of cash inside! He said it didn't make sense to have a nice purse like that with no money inside, so she had her first wad! She was now a member of the Wad Squad. He would laugh so hard every time she pulled it out. She was the apple of his eye. I want you to hear from her what her Papa means to her.

George Thomas Halsey, Jr. - the most influential man in my life, point blank period. From the time I was old enough to recognize, my Papa was my absolute biggest fan. In his eyes, I could do no wrong and I felt absolutely perfect whenever I was around him-so much so that I'd be confused when people actually disliked me in later years. Either way, my grandfather's support was limitless. His love was unconditional. He cried tears of pride at every dance and every piano recital. He always seemed impressed by my mental aptitude. He enjoyed that I read books incessantly until about age 12. He promoted my dreams of becoming an archaeologist, an ice skater and an anesthesiologist all within months of each other. My Papa helped me to become an independent thinker. While he laughed at the people waking up early to go to work, I laughed at the kids waking up early to attend public school since I was being home schooled. We found it cool to wake up at 12noon with no real place to be or urgency in our uprising. I actually remember arriving a little late to some of my sessions with my instructor because we had been out to eat.

Papa was amused by the fact that I'd completed all the high school requirements for our state by age 16. He encouraged my teacher's suggestion of starting college at such a young age, simply because I could. I attended N.C. A&T State University, the very same school where he and Nana met. After receiving my BFA in Professional Theater at age 20, Papa continued to support my dreams as I pursued higher education. Never once did he tell me to go to school so I could get a "good job," but instead so that I'd be equipped with all the training necessary to develop a successful singing/acting career. My family NEVER missed a play performance, not in Greensboro and not in Gainesville, FL as I attended graduate school at the University of Florida. Nothing was as gratifying as seeing his smiling face in the audience. I could always spot him, handkerchief in hand to catch the silent tears he'd let fall as he watched. Unfortunately, my grandfather would become ill days before I was scheduled to return to NC for a semester-long internship in 2008. I could have accepted a number of theater internships in "better cities," but I opted for one in Greensboro because God told me I needed to be close to my family (at the time, Papa was in good health). I was elated to spend a couple months at home and never thought twice about the 'why.'

Papa wouldn't be around to see me receive my MFA in Acting at age 23. He wouldn't help me move to Atlanta in 2010 to pursue my singing/acting career or see me perform in my first role in a new city. He wouldn't be in attendance at any concert I sang backup for, or see my first role in a movie (but he always loved him some Tyler Perry). He won't walk me down the aisle, see me accept my Oscar's or Grammy's, give me marriage advice or welcome his first great grandchild into the world. He won't witness the purchase of my first home or be able to enjoy the success I intend to have, thanks to the dream he instilled in my heart. Even though he's not physically here, I know he's somewhere smiling and watching over me. He sees my challenges, my victories, my downfalls, my heartaches & my growth - all the while, he's grinning & saying, "My Booba" and knowing this, makes my heart smile.

-Kislyck Mykela Halsey

Chapter 14
Final Days with George

"The first time I knew of [George and Ruth], they were in a magazine. I saw this ritzy couple, with all of these fabulous cars. They were presented as the epitome of what Black folks wanted to become. I read the article at least 5 times because I was a poor country boy and we barely had two pairs of shoes. They were really like figments of my imagination. "What in the world did they do?' I thought. "How in the world did they do it?" There were 'those' people—out there like a Bill Cosby or something. Anybody who is "SOMEbody"...that was the category I placed them in.

–Bishop George Brooks

As I sat down to write this book, I couldn't do it without the help of my pastor and dear friend, Bishop George Brooks of the Mt. Zion Baptist Church in Greensboro. He has been here with us through the thick and thin; through the ugly and the happy. How we met Pastor Brooks is a book in and of itself.

George was in his late forties. We were flying every year to Hawaii, and one trip, while vacationing there, he got sick on the island. So we brought him back and ran some tests. Doctors told us that George had diabetes. But that didn't stop him. He did what he had to do and got back out on the road. A few months later, while in our condo in Hilton Head, he got sick again. Doctors decided to take out his thyroid at that point, so he started taking medicine for that as well. George was a trooper. He would try to handle business like he had always done, but I could tell that it was beginning to take a toll on him.

Over a period of 8 years, George experienced a gradual decline in his health. Next thing we knew, doctors started talking about his heart. So we got George a heart doctor, and they went to work on his heart to make sure everything was stable. By the time he accepted the fact that he had diabetes, it was a little too late. George loved to eat whatever he wanted to eat, and unfortunately, he had messed himself up before medical intervention could take place. One time he said the diabetes was so bad he couldn't feel his feet. It was becoming overwhelming. We didn't know what to do. Karen decided to seek God. That's how we ended up with Bishop & First Lady Brooks at Mt. Zion Baptist Church.

⌁ MEETING BISHOP BROOKS ⌁
"My dad started getting sick and I felt like he needed deliverance. I didn't know what deliverance really meant, but in my mind, deliverance was casting out demons or praying until the spirits were out. So I was ready for warfare. I put on a sweat suit and I told my mom, 'We're going for warfare.' The appointment was set. And off we went."
-Karen Halsey

We didn't know why George was experiencing this ongoing sickness from one thing to another, so Karen assumed that someone had cast a spell on her father. After all, we were always traveling to foreign countries and we were eating in so many cities, it wouldn't shock me if someone who didn't like George plotted to destroy him. Some people are like that. They want nothing else in life but to bring you down. And unlike me, George was very trusting. I didn't trust many people's cooking. I didn't eat off of anybody's plate. George, on the other hand, ate everything. And Karen, knowing her father, went on a mission to get her father well by any means necessary. She asked her hairdresser about a pastor in town that she could go and talk to about this private matter.

Because most of the people knew us in Greensboro, she wanted a pastor to respect our privacy, and not expose our situation. George Brooks was recommended to us, and Karen made the initial phone call.

When we arrived to the church, we sat outside the conference room waiting for Bishop Brooks to invite us in. When I asked Bishop about this meeting, this is what he said:

"The day came when I was to meet the people I had always admired from afar. It's really one of those days you probably only live once or twice in your life. But when they walked in, I wasn't intimidated nor afraid. When I sat down with them, our conversation was better than I expected. They were not just cool, they were really cool; down-to-earth; laid back-cool. For me, this was a shock because you expect for people with private planes and who share rooms with Presidents to carry a certain kind of heir with them. But this was not my experience. Not in the least bit!"

Bishop would later tell us stories about how he came to know of us, but it didn't matter who he thought we were at that point. We just needed help. He didn't know what we wanted, and we thought we did. The initial meeting became the introduction of a lifelong friendship. He cared about us as people. He listened to us with a pastoral heart, and he guided us through "real deliverance." We came expecting a high emotional exorcism. We left with the peace of God.

Pastor Brooks quickly told us that we would need to walk through this journey together. We agreed. He prayed with us and committed to pastoring us long before we joined his church. He brought us books on discipleship and Christianity, and he would go over the basics with us until we understood what he was talking about. The man has a gift of teaching. Anyone who cares to listen, he will give you his time. The first time he came to our home, it felt like he was family. George was sitting in his chair and Pastor Brooks would just listen to us, talk with us—for hours at a time—laugh with us, and eat with us.

A few months later, around George's birthday, we were sitting at the kitchen table and George made a family announcement. We were going to join Bishop Brooks' church. That's right. At the end of service, we were going to walk up together as a family and join. The news was unbelievable to me because George was always a private guy; especially when it came to his spiritual side. He didn't let many people in, but apparently, he took to Bishop Brooks and his life began to change right before my very eyes.

This is our Bishop and First Lady Brooks

⌁ SICKNESS IN ST. LOUIS ⌁

"George was a calming force. He had the innate ability in any situation to speak to you, and you could literally feel serenity and tranquility easing in. He was the kind of guy that you wanted on your side if you were in a tough situation.

- Bishop Brooks

The year before we said goodbye, we drove to St. Louis for a conference. By this point, we were active members of our church, and Bishop Brooks was trying to talk George into becoming a deacon. But we still had our business and it was thriving. Well, the first day we arrived, George started feeling a little sick. Immediately, I decided to take him to the hospital because there was no way I could work knowing he was not well. The ambulance came. It wasn't a major emergency. When they got there, he was responsive and stable. The next morning, doctors told us that he was on a respirator and they asked us for permission to resuscitate if necessary! We were blown away. He had only had a stomachache when we left him the night before. We later found out that they had given him too much fluid and his body couldn't handle all of it. When Karen and I walked into the room, we saw George hooked up to a respirator—his head was like twice his normal size. He was so swollen with fluid that he didn't even look like himself. We walked out of the room, a tear rolled down our eyes and we looked at each other in the waiting room in disbelief.

"I need a Bible," I said.

We found one in the waiting room, held hands, and began to pray for his healing. The prognosis from the doctors was not good, but we believed in the Almighty.

That same night, our friends Rick and Sue Lynn, Harvey and Bobby, visited us in the hospital to provide support and care. Rick and Sue Lynn moved us into the hospital hotel, and told us not to worry about food, lodging or anything. They paid for everything. This was, once again, another time that we discovered that this was more than a business.

Seven days later, George was still on the respirator. We ended up staying in Missouri for a month. I wouldn't stop praying. I kept believing that God would work a miracle. The doctors weren't very hopeful. But I chose not to receive it. All my life, I was accustomed to people telling me who I was supposed to be, and I didn't receive it then; so what makes you think I am going to accept it now? God had been too good to us to leave us in this place. So we prayed. My pastor prayed. Karen got her herbs together (she had been practicing herbal medicine for years before this time) and rubbed them on her father. Mucus was being pumped out of his body every day. From the looks of things, George was not going to come back to us.

But on the eighth day, he woke up! He was laughing and smiling and thanking all of the nurses for taking care of him. He never knew exactly what had transpired, but he was thanking everyone for everything. The nurses and doctors had seen a walking miracle. We put some of the herbs in his water to stop the fluid from building up and it worked. God was still showing me that prayer works!

The next barrier was getting George home. The hospital told us that George couldn't fly or drive by regular means of transportation, so the only way to return home would be by medical plane. It costs $20,000 to transport him on a medical plane. We prayed and the blessings continued to flow. Before George was flown home, we had to find a place for him to stay with the proper medical support. The hospitals wouldn't accept him in Greensboro, and we couldn't take him back to our house. But we finally found a nursing home that would accept him.

When he finally got home, he struggled with walking a bit but he refused to depend on a walker. He could certainly walk without one but he was more stable with it. If we went somewhere for a long period of time, we would have to get a wheelchair and push him. George Halsey did not like that. We were trained in this business to never give up. We expected him to walk, and soon after, he got up and walked!

George survived another year and a half before he had the stroke on August 25. He was recovering, laughing, and joking again. He never recovered 100 %, but he was still making appearances here and there. From time to time, Bishop Brooks would come and check in with us. One time, Bishop Brooks got down on his knees and washed George's feet. It was the ultimate act of humility, and it touched us in the deepest way; that he would serve us in this manner meant the world to us. But it wasn't just Bishop Brooks who did this. Everyone who loved George was so concerned about us. The phone calls never stopped. The offers to help us with our business didn't stop. It felt good to know that people had your back every step of the way.

On that night in August, no one could've prepared me for this final roller-coaster dip. We were lying in the bed together listening to First Lady Michelle Obama speak. We were in shock and disbelief. It seemed we would finally have a Black President. This was history in the making. George was so excited!

"Do you think we are really going to have a Black President?" he asked.

"I think he's got it, George!"

"Hmph..." he thought, as he imagined the possibility.

We both talked the night away until, finally, George dozed off to sleep. A few hours later-- it was about 3AM--I got up to use the bathroom and I saw his foot hanging off the bed. It didn't "feel" right so I walked over on his side and pushed him a little.

"George, George! What's the matter with you?"

He didn't respond.

"George, George! Are you alright?"

He moved a little bit but he didn't respond in words. I called for Karen and she called 911. Everything from there happened fast but so slow at the same time. The ambulance was there in no time. I could hear the clock ticking on the wall, and all I could do was pray. When the ambulance arrived, I noticed they didn't do the same things for George that they did when his mom had a stroke at our house a few years prior. Their procedure was different this time.

They rushed him to the hospital. I rode with him and Karen followed. We waited and waited and waited. As I waited, my mind flashed back over all the years of joy that George had brought me. All of our dreams had come true, and he was determined to make me the happiest woman in the world. I thought of us walking up to join our church. I thought of Karen's birth. I thought of our granddaughter. I thought of our friends, our team, our dogs---everything you could think of was running through my mind. Our marriage of 51 years. I thought about the things that really mattered. It didn't matter how much money we had in the bank, or how many clothes and furs and diamonds we had. I was too busy counting the real memories of love, family, and God as I stared at the wall in that waiting room.

Finally, the doctor escorted us to the back. I knew it wasn't good. I felt it in the pit of my stomach. He brought us into the room where George was. He was alive, but he was not responding very much. The stroke had damaged 2/3 of his brain. I couldn't stand to see my husband like that, so I had to walk out. I told Karen to handle the doctors and I stepped out. It wasn't very long until God transitioned my first and only love from this life to eternal life.

∽ SOMEHOW, GOD KEPT US ∽

Karen and I didn't know what to do, at first. We were surrounded by love—both spiritual and natural—but we had to deal with what life would be like when we got home. We were such a close family unit, we couldn't imagine dinner without him. Everyone knew we were a tight family; whenever you saw one of us, you saw all of us. And now, the man of the house wasn't coming home with us. We just didn't know how to feel. Somehow, the funeral arrangements were made. Programs were designed. Flowers were purchased. Food was prepared. But I don't remember much of anything. People flew from every part of the world. Thousands showed up for George's Homegoing service. Bishop Brooks eulogized him in the most honorable way. I was present but I wasn't really aware. I was kind of numb. I didn't know what to do or say when George left us. It was like a piece of my heart died with him when he went on to be with the Lord. It felt like my mother's death, but deeper. It felt like my father's death, but closer.

Not a day goes by that I don't think of him. Not a month goes by that I don't find a trace of George around the house somewhere. This is what I consider the most important part of this story. It's not OVER!

You see, I married a man that built something that we could continue. The dream is not over. He left us a legacy that still lives; one that can be passed on to our daughter and son, her daughter and her (future) children and so on and so on. It never ends. George's biggest dream was to leave a legacy. When he showed the plan, he would tell people with tears in his eyes that if he died he didn't want us wanting for anything, he wanted to leave us with something that would continue for generations. God gave him the desires of his heart.

One day when we were cleaning out one of his drawers we found this:

We didn't recognize the scripture so we looked it up in the Message Bible, it said:

Then Jesus arrived from Nazareth, anointed by God with the Holy Spirit, ready for action. He went through the country helping people and healing everyone who was beaten down by the devil. He was able to do all this because God was with Him.

I wonder if George knew when he wrote down that scripture that he was describing himself. Everyone who knew him knew that he was anointed by God. He went

Copy of his handwriting with scripture

through the country helping people who were beat down. He helped those that were beaten by discrimination, depression and low self esteem. George made sure that everyone he met felt important and valuable. He did what sometimes seemed impossible, but he was able to do all this because God was with him. He did not leave this earth until his mission was accomplished. And while I would love to have him by my side right now, I know for sure, that God wanted him more. I married a man that did whatever it took to get the job done, it didn't matter if he was raised without his parents or if he was afraid. It didn't matter that he was a black man in a country that would sometimes reject him. It didn't matter if he was shy or tired, used, abused, talked about—it didn't matter if he was sick and weak, he would get up, smile, laugh and dream.

His dream still lives in us, Karen, Kissy, John and Me!

HIS DREAM STILL LIVES........

The entire family at the Grahams' family reunion. Left to right: Karen, Kissy, George, me and John.

Chapter 15
Final Words....Keep Dreaming

Money is great but it's only a tool. You exchange money for goods and services. The more you have, the more goods you can provide. It doesn't make you more than or less than, it's just a necessary tool. And when you don't have any [money], life can be very difficult. If you find a way to live a successful life, then give it all you've got.

-George Halsey

Like George said, "Give it all you've got!" I've learned a few things in this life, nobody owes you a living, your successes or failures are directly related to what you do or don't do. We can't choose our parents nor how we were raised, but we can choose the direction we take. Everyone will have situations and obstacles to overcome. These can be as different as the individual, but no matter what they are, these things don't define you. You are capable of changing anything in your life if you want to badly. I don't accept excuses. People who take responsibility for their actions are the real winners in life. You've got to meet your situations and obstacles head on, understanding that there are no guarantees – Give it all you've got! It's never too late nor too early to begin. Time plays no favorites and will pass whether you get moving or sit still. Now is the time to take control of your life. DREAM BIG DREAMS! A wise young woman once told me that if your dream doesn't require God to make it come true, it isn't big enough. DREAM BIG DREAMS! Risks must be taken. The greatest hazard in life is to risk nothing. The person who risks nothing... does nothing...

has nothing and is nothing. They may avoid suffering and sorrow but they will not learn, feel, change, grow, love, nor live.

Believe In Yourself!! And I'll see YOU at The TOP!!